G000245806

EMOTIONS
Experiences in Existential Psychotherapy and Life

Freddie Strasser

Duckworth

First published in 1999 by
Gerald Duckworth & Co. Ltd.
61 Frith Street, London W1V 5TA
Tel: 0171 434 4242
Fax: 0171 434 4420
Email: enquiries@duckworth-publishers.co.uk

ISBN 0 7156 2837 2

Typeset by Derek Doyle & Associates, Mold
Printed in Great Britain by
Redwood Books Ltd, Trowbridge

Contents

Foreword   vii
Preface   ix

Introduction   1

1. Basic Assumptions   7
2. Emotions   23
3. Anger   35
4. Fear and Anxiety   53
5. Guilt   71
6. Sadness   85
7. Shame   105

Supervision   118

8. Joy   121
9. Hate   139

10. Epilogue (Jacob)   155

Graphs   166
References   169
Index   173

To Alcaryv

Foreword

How difficult (if not impossible) it is to make sense of emotions. After centuries of speculation and theorising by philosophers and psychologists, no model has emerged that satisfies all the various observations and lived experiences that human beings associate with the general label of 'emotions'. To read the plentiful, if not over-abundant, literature that has been generated in the attempt to capture the meaning and function of emotions provokes the intellectual equivalent of stepping through a minefield so vast and dangerous that those who make the attempt, while undoubtedly courageous, might also be judged to be more than a little foolhardy. I must admit that when Freddie Strasser first mentioned to me that he was contemplating embarking upon 'a little book on emotions', my initial reaction was to seek to dissuade him from the enterprise. I am very pleased to report that he did not take my advice. This book stands as witness both to my error of judgement and to his unique wisdom.

This is not yet another text promising a solution to the dilemma caused by emotions. Far more usefully, and importantly, Freddie Strasser has succeeded in providing his readers with a descriptive exploration of a variety of distinct, yet common, human emotions – such as anger, fear, sadness and joy. As a psychotherapist, the chosen landscape for such explorations is made up of the accounts provided him by his clients. These are simply, and movingly, conveyed to the reader in a direct and immediate fashion such that the therapeutic tendency toward platitude and mystification is expertly avoided. Indeed, Freddie Strasser's willingness to include several of his clients' own commentaries on their experience of therapy with him allows the emergence of uncommon insights and an all too rare entry into the lived world of the client that few therapists are brave – and humble – enough to offer to their readers. It is an invaluable privilege – and pleasure – to encounter people, and not 'case histories', throughout the book.

The deeply human(e) qualities which permeate throughout the text are further exemplified in Freddie Strasser's willingness to include pertinent material on 'felt emotions' drawn from significant moments in his own personal life experiences. This step serves to both underscore and extend the descriptive analyses provided. More than this, however, these powerful accounts provide the means for readers to 'feel', as well as consider, the emotions under discussion. As readers of this book will soon enough discover for themselves, Freddie Strasser's approach to the exploration of emotions is deeply influenced by his understanding of existential-phenomenological theory as applied to psychotherapy and counselling. Once again, his avoidance of jargon permits an uncustomary and rewarding clarity to emerge.

This is, first and foremost, a highly readable and accessible text. It is also both original and (if I may employ a decidedly over-used term) profound. Freddie Strasser's distinction between reflected and unreflected emotions provides a significant contribution to therapeutic thought and practice and I can only hope that further elaborations on this important insight will be forthcoming in due course. One final comment: while I remain very much in agreement with the many pertinent points raised by Freddie Strasser and am greatly touched by his kindness in his assertion in the preface that I, personally, should be recognised as having played some meaningful role in the development and explication of the various ideas presented herein, I cannot accept this conclusion. Whatever plaudits and recognition it deserves (and I sincerely hope will attain) is due entirely to his inspired and innovative ways of thinking about, and working with, emotions. The book not only accomplishes the task of communicating the author's views and conclusions on the topic, it also serves to stimulate the readers' own perspectives, and thereby succeeds in illuminating their own encounters with this quintessential expression of 'being-human'.

Professor Ernesto Spinelli
School of Psychotherapy and Counselling at Regent's College
London, UK

Preface

The aim of this book is to convey in a commonsensical manner my own and my clients' experiences with emotions in therapy and in the world. It is targeted at a wide range of readers, including psychotherapists, psychologists, students and trainees, as well as those who are interested in the subject of emotions.

The reader may discover several notions in this book which have not previously been explored in the same fashion elsewhere. My own belief is that whatever there may be in this book that is novel is the result of a mutual exploration between Ernesto Spinelli and myself. I could not have written this book in the manner it is written had I not received his unstinting support. From the book's inception onwards, Ernesto encouraged, guided and supplied me with ideas to complement my own experience. For all these, I am deeply indebted to him. I am grateful to Emmy van Deurzen-Smith for launching me on my existential journey.

The book is dedicated to Alcaryv, which is the acronym for the names of my daughters Alison, Carolyn, and Yvonne – all three of them are involved in psychotherapy. The book is about experiencing emotions and all three, in their own particular way, have contributed, sometimes knowingly and sometimes unknowingly. From their unrelenting, honest and open discussions, and with their devotion to both my project and to myself, I have learned and benefited greatly and I am grateful to them for all of these things.

I am also deeply grateful to Jacob and Kane and to all my clients and supervisees from whom I gained knowledge and insights. I particularly thank Alison Strasser and Claire Schrader for their contributions in writing up their own experiences as co-supervisor and supervisee respectively.

I express special thanks to Amelia, Barbara and Sophie, not only for their diligent and understanding work in therapy, but also for their courage and openness in writing their own accounts about their experiences in therapy. I also extend my thanks to Cherry, my client, for her devotion to therapy, her hard work, and giving me the privilege of sharing her emotions and her journey in her explorations of her world-view. Lynn I thank for helping me in my struggles to keep my moods on an even keel while writing this book.

To John Karter, who edited the book, I express my gratitude for his patience, advice, and enthusiasm; Karen Dixon Weixel for her relentless academic support; and Paul Burg for his unfailing help in the preparation of the manuscript.

Finally, Robin Baird-Smith, the publisher, was always ready to help me with my problems and encouraged me in my work. He was always ready to listen and give me his unbiased and constructive criticism and advice. For all this, I express my thanks and appreciation. I am indebted to Martin Rynja for his untiring and understanding work in the final editing of this book.

Introduction

To begin with, I have to introduce myself as a practising psychotherapist and counsellor. Although I am not a theoretician, my guiding line in therapy, nonetheless, emanates from a philosophical influence – phenomenology. This philosophical standpoint argues that things can be investigated, not only by conventional scientific methods, but also by simply experiencing and describing them. Edmund Husserl, a German mathematician turned philosopher, called this attitude an attempt to return 'To the things themselves'. This means, to rediscover an open-minded or 'naïve' contact with the world.

This standpoint is in direct opposition to scientific causal research that employs hard, analytical, reductionist methods to overcome our 'falsifications' of our perceptual objects. I certainly do not doubt the validity of scientific analysis in its endeavours to research the natural phenomena. Yet, in human relationships, including that of the therapist-client, I feel more comfortable with simply attempting an approach that focuses upon experiencing and describing what is happening between us. By moving intuitively and, as far as possible, uncontaminated by prejudices, I progress towards the 'things themselves'. In this context, the therapeutic relationship is an engagement in discourse between clients and therapists, an exploration of experiences: between the clients themselves, between clients and therapists, and between clients and their outside world.

The description of experiences in this 'naïve' fashion is the theme that will guide this book. The book began life as an objective, analytical survey of my therapeutic experiences with the different emotions of my clients. As the book progressed, however, it gradually became clear that, both in therapy and in the writing of this work, I could not extricate myself from my own emotions. Unwittingly, in a strange and imperceptible way, the book is in part my own story.

Many valuable books and treatises have been written about the *theory* of emotions. Even so, it is difficult to find a unified and precise definition for this nomenclature. The difficulty in defining 'emotion' arises from divergences in the underpinning of various competing

1

theories. My intention is not to present yet another emotional and motivational theory, nor to give a definitive definition for emotions.

My objective is to reveal the intimate relational nature of emotions in human encounters; in short, to reveal emotion in *practice*. Since Sartre (1948) there is very little pertinent literature that explicitly discusses the importance of emotions as part of both life and in the (existential) psychotherapeutic environment. Furthermore, in this book the distinction between 'reflective' and 'unreflective' emotions in therapy, as far as I know, is examined in detail for the first time.

Thus, I recount my own experiences with the emotional experiences of clients, how these connect with my own issues, and to what extent my own issues interconnect positively or negatively in therapeutic encounters. I also discuss how each emotion discussed in the text is closely related to other emotions and how these connect with other aspects of human experience. This, in turn, will convey to the reader how the impact of even an insignificant emotion can open clients to re-examine how they exist in the world. The book also analyses the common aspects of emotions which manifest themselves between different clients, and clients and myself. I also draw attention to the vast differences that exist between individuals' emotional expressions and their behavioural consequences. The sameness, the universal commonalties as well as the uniqueness of each individual is the theme that will guide our exploration.

My view of therapy and counselling is predicated by that which I have learned from my clients, my students and from my own life experiences. Supervising trainee psychotherapists has also been a rich source of learning. Lastly and importantly, my work in therapy is influenced by notions and theories, which I have studied and considered over many years. These have made me the person that I am.

I call myself an existentially oriented therapist. Existential therapy is only one of many orientations in the vast psychotherapeutic field, which, according to Richie Herink, counts some two hundred and fifty orientations (1986). Their protagonists are usually protective of their models. (Whilst the differences may sometimes be vast, I believe that are many common denominators within all therapies.) The traditional Freudian psychoanalytic approach maintains that a cure for the patient would take place when a repressed complex emerges from the unconscious to the conscious. Freud said: 'where id was ego shall be' (1973:112). In divergence to this, the humanistic approach would say that awareness itself is curative (Perls:1959). Behavioural and cognitive therapists, however, argue that cure rests in modification of behaviour patterns. And contrary to the large variety of theories, Richard Bandler and John Grinder, the originators of neurolinguistic programming (NLP therapy), generally disagreed about the importance of a certain school of thinking. They studied and researched the outcome of therapeutic endeavours of the main psychological models and demonstrated that, irrespective of the theoretical background, the result of the therapeutic outcome depended much more on the charismatic character of the therapist and less on theories (1979).

While I call myself an existential therapist, I would by no means maintain that I rigidly adhere to a single approach, and that I have not been influenced by many other than existential thinkers – although this does not preclude the fact that I maintain certain basic assumptions. I know from my own experience that applying the basic existential tenets to practice is best suited to my practical work, but I admit that other models could be as effective as ours. I am also aware that some of the basic phenomenological and existential notions can be debated. But in all I believe that the existential model of human interaction has the clearest guidelines for understanding the issues that concern psychotherapy.

There are abundant examples of divergences even between those therapists who profess to be existentially minded. It is interesting to quote Ernesto Spinelli from his 'Réculer pour mieux sauter' (1999), where he cautions of the existing tendency to assume that all existentially influenced philosophers, or psychologists are 'all really just existential thinkers and practitioners'. Existential therapy consists of a variety of input from different philosophers to differing psychotherapeutic approaches.

This book is designed to illustrate how I work in therapy and how this way of working relates to emotions. The first and the second chapters describe my basic assumptions relating to emotions. Each following chapter will focus on one emotion. Anger, fear, guilt, love, sadness, shame, and joy will all tell their own story. These will first be discussed in terms of my own experiences, coming from events in my life. Relating the same emotion to a client's case history will follow this. This is then commented upon by clients, and the chapters also contain the clients' own perceptions of the therapy. Each client is thoroughly acquainted with the contents of their relevant contribution and gave permission to publish. Nevertheless, the names and sometimes the circumstances of individuals have been changed.

The first chapter describes in detail the underpinning structure of my work in therapy, while the second chapter is about emotions, the differences between reflective (aware) and unreflective (unaware) emotions, and explores how these play a vital role in therapy and in the assessment of our world-views. Case vignettes demonstrate this and also the notion that we are never without emotions and that emotions invariably denote something. The third, fourth, fifth, sixth and seventh chapters will explore clients' and my own experiences and attitudes towards a particular emotion.

The eighth chapter introduces the notion of supervision, which is an accepted practice in the profession. Chapter eight describes joy in the context of four sessions of one-to-one supervision with Claire Schrader, an experienced drama therapist. She felt frustrated with one of her clients for prematurely ending her therapy course. Claire decided to expand her horizons and try to look at her work from another point of view, in this case from an existential perspective. This chapter is also about my own exploration of the emotion of joy and how joy reacquainted me with my own world-view. Claire describes her experiences with her client in the context of her supervision experiences with me.

Chapter nine introduces the concept of co-supervision. Many times, in highly charged therapeutic encounters, even the most experienced counsellors or psychotherapists overlook or misunderstand things that can be of importance. Discussing problematic issues with a trusting colleague can clarify even the most glaring discrepancies. My daughter Alison is a psychotherapist in Australia and she and I were very lucky in having been able to develop a trusting and honest, defence-free co-counselling relationship. Alison and I wrote a book together about time-limited existential therapy (1997), and developed the skill to co-supervise each other. In this chapter, I introduce the notion of co-counselling and Alison describes the 'paradox of hate', the ambivalence between hate and love in the context of the supervision.

In the tenth chapter, I outline how emotions and issues interconnect all the time. This is a chapter about Jacob. He was declared mentally handicapped at a very young age and has kept this label right to this present day. In spite of this, or because of it, he was able to describe and explore his predicament with clarity, and conciseness. He was also able to go to 'the things themselves' in the most uncontaminated way. I always maintain that I learn most from my clients and supervisees, and I must include in this category Jacob. In his spontaneous and instinctive philosophy of life, he introduced me to many important notions and facets of my own being that I was not aware of. In this chapter, I compare his issues with mine and how our world-view interconnects with all emotions and other givens in our life.

This book will describe how to employ clients' experiences of emotions as a tool in facilitating individuals to work through their chain of emotions and enable them to link these with their value systems. It will also help them to connect with their entrenched coping mechanisms and their self-identification or self-esteem. Through this process, it is shown how clients also become aware of their limitations, as well as the potential to make their own decisions. They have the opportunity to explore their world-view.

What is meant by 'world-view'? The first and the second chapters deal with this question in detail. It is sufficient to say here that our 'world-view' encompasses all those facets of our existence that enable us to understand how we exist in this world. This is the world that each of us perceives and makes us behave in our unique, idiosyncratic manner.

If a world-view illuminates what people are and if emotions reveal this world-view then, if we therapists have the capacity to listen to clients' and our own emotions, we can soon become acquainted with our own and the clients' world-views. As I have stated earlier, we are never without emotions. We reveal ourselves all the time through our emotions, not only verbally but also in our body posture and body language. We have only to learn how to listen and how to attend to them. If we learn how to listen to our own emotions, we can also learn how to attend to others' emotions. If we cannot attend honestly to our own world-view, to our true motivations, and to our true value systems, it is futile even to try to understand others. Needless to say, the ability to detect others' world-views also carries a danger of misusing this knowledge and to manipulate others. This is, however, an ethical issue, which is outside the scope of this book.

1

Basic Assumptions

In existential therapy one generally uses empathic therapeutic skills. Such skills were adopted from Carl Rogers (1980), Fritz Pearls (1959), and others. It is, furthermore, also a conglomeration of many philosophical notions taken from Kierkegaard (1844), Husserl (1975), Heidegger (1962) and many others. Spinelli wrote about the question of diversity, when he spoke how, for example, Friedrich Nietzsche provided considerable stimulus to existential-phenomenological enquiry. It would, however, be wrong to suggest, in Spinelli's words, 'that Nietzsche was some sort of crypto-existentialist or "nothing other than" an existentialist' (1999). Spinelli continues to argue that similar arguments could be made of Kierkegaard and of many others.

Existential philosophy and phenomenology need to be given a working definition for the purpose of this experientially orientated book. Ultimately, existential philosophy proposes a set of initial features as to what it means to be a human being. The word existence has its roots in the Latin *existere*, which can be translated as 'to stand out'. We stand out and we create our world between birth and death in a continuous process – in the face of all the limitations of the world. For the very essence of this approach is that it seeks to analyse and portray the human being – whether in art or literature, philosophy or psychology – on a level which undercuts the old dilemma of materialism versus idealism. Existentialism, in short, is the endeavour to understand man by cutting below the cleavage between subject and object that has bedevilled Western thought and science since shortly after the Renaissance (May 1983:49).

In order to investigate how we create and exist in this world, existentialism employs a particular method of investigation. Known as phenomenology it subjectively interprets 'things'. This interpretation excludes objective reality and focuses on human existence on the basis of phenomena. In other words, how we create and exist in the world is explained through the method of experiencing the phenomena. In short, it claims that scientific explanation falsifies the real nature of human experience.

Edmund Husserl was the founder of the philosophical movement known as phenomenology. He attempted to develop an alternative scientific explanation which excluded the Cartesian dichotomy between body and mind. Husserl focused on subjective interpretations as according to him phenomena cannot be described without the inseparable relationship between human consciousness and the world. Human consciousness is always directed towards the world to give a meaning to it. That is to say, if I become aware of my anger, then my attention is directed towards something or someone. This also means that I am attributing some meaning to this something or someone (1975:10).

The object in this method is best characterised by Fell, who quotes the well-known French phenomenologist Merleau-Ponty's: 'It is a philosophy ... whose entire effort is to discover [a] naïve contact with the world' (1965:226). This is achieved by the attempt to set aside, or what is called 'bracketing', our biases and preconceived judgements and to be open to our immediate experience. Thus, phenomenology seeks to describe phenomena, instead of analysing and explaining them. In so doing it returns the investigator to the 'things themselves'.

Needless to say, this is disputed by natural and other sciences where it is argued that our natural perceptions are not adequate for investigating things as we perceive them. Science needs to analyse and reduce matter to its smallest constituents to arrive at an objective truth. The existentially oriented therapies, however, claim that phenomenological method of a 'bracketed' investigation is more effective for examination of human relationships than the scientific one. For phenomenologists bracketing means to suspend our expectation prejudices to focus on the primary data of our experiences.

Many also argue that suspending our prejudices is practically impossible. Yet, in spite of such arguments, my experience is that the attempt to divest ourselves of prejudices in therapy is important and useful, even if we know that we cannot entirely achieve it. As I do not profess to be a theoretician, I rely mostly on my experience with clients, which tells me that the main notions of the existential paradigm are most conducive to working with clients.

Indeed, one of the most significant experiences I have gained by working with clients is that the act of being with the client epitomises

interpersonal relationships,
values and their polarities,
belief our meaning and behaviour systems,
sedimentation of the belief and behaviour system,
aspirations and freedom of choice.

In short, our world-view is the expression of the sum total of our particular way of being with or engaging in the world.

For example, a client presents a problem that, although she thinks that she is extrovert by nature, she is unable to express herself in front of other people. She becomes aware in therapy that she has a rigid belief system based on an unyielding assumption that the only and best way for her to exist in the world is by humility. Thus she clearly demonstrates her value system in respect of this issue: that humility is always a positive and showing off is always a negative attribute. Clearly, her self-esteem depends on achieving her aspiration to be modest and she restricts her desire to be in any way extrovert. In order to escape from the threat of being rejected, she either withdraws or drinks when meeting 'other' people. All this is accompanied by various emotions and physical expressions, such as body language, which also disclose the client's values and other particular ways in which she exists in the world.

The revelation of all these emotions and expressions and her ability to choose her attitude towards her belief system and self-concept constitutes this client's world-view. Needless to say, her world-view could have been disclosed just as well through other aspects of her being in the world. For example, one of her other strategies for survival was her ability to change from an extrovert person into a studious, academic one. In focusing on this aspect of her being – whether in a positive or negative sense – she also disclosed her values, self-esteem and world-view.

Although the outlined structure of being is only an abstract representation of how we exist in the world, it provides the therapist with an anchor. In therapy, there are two human beings, the client and the therapist, engaged in discourse, a relationship in which both are intertwined, having the same limitations in the world; they both face individual decisions how to respond to these constraints.

In addition, during the therapeutic interaction, clients will also have the opportunity to absorb and learn a dialectic mode of approach. In other words, clients will become acquainted with a method of questioning and challenging their own assumptions and contradictions. In exploring one issue, clients may soon become aware how to deal with other issues. All issues are, in any case, linked to each other. Clients will have to deal with their own issues between sessions and after the end of the course of therapy. Therapy is not about clients' total analysis, as some issues will always remain, emerge, or re-emerge in their life.

A client presented his problems of insomnia, depression, and the meaninglessness of his life. In therapy, we explored his anger which was directed at his partner who was 'responsible' for the demise of their business. It soon became apparent that his aspirations in life were intrinsically connected to his belief that success in business was everything. His self-esteem was totally dependent on the success of their business. When his partner embezzled his fortune and absconded, his whole world lost its meaning. All other meanings in his life, such as spirituality, family and children, receded into the background and utter depression ensued. This client could only begin to challenge himself, when he became aware of his rigid value system. And then he could explore other meanings in life.

Usually it takes a lot more effort and many series of insights before substantial changes take place. Nonetheless, the mere realisation of their world-view can evoke insights in clients; and this in turn can create an impetus to change in the clients' attitudes. In this case, the client's questioning of 'do I have to invest all my meaning in material well-being?' represented in itself a slight shift in his life.

THE STRUCTURE OF BEING

The structure of our being in the world, described in this section, attempts to embody some of those universal givens which the world imposes upon us and some of the givens that we humans create to survive and to find a secure place in this world. The uncertainty and inconsistency of the world spawn responses such as the creation of values, self-esteem, and other givens to secure our place in this universe.

Although individuals create their own individual strategies for survival, we all need to respond to these givens. Some existential authors, such as Hans Cohn, describe those universal givens that limit our life as 'ontological', whereas the individual responses are 'ontic' characteristics (1997). The way I work with a client is influenced by the structure of being in which I see myself existing in the world which helps me to connect empathetically with the client's issues. In this relationship, clients examine parts of their world-view and their inherent ambivalences.

Uncertainty Uncertainty and inconsistency characterise our existence from the day we are born to the day we die. The awareness of the inconsistency and unpredictability of each moment of living lurks in the background or foreground of most human activities.

This is a universal given or, as some authors call it, one of the 'ontological' characteristics of the world to which we all respond in our own idiosyncratic manner. Furthermore, we can accept that each person will experience this uncertainty in his or her particular manner, not only unlike us, but also differently at different times. This is the uniqueness of our existence.

In therapy, we try to establish a safe environment and provide clients with firm boundaries within which they can rely on consistency and predictability. This consists of a contractual agreement plus the setting of the consulting room, a non-intrusive place that is conducive to this confidential encounter. Time, fees and, very importantly, the degree of commitment of both parties needs to be agreed upon.

A note of caution, however. Sometimes therapists overlook the real purpose of this safe environment and, therefore, may miss the fact that the objective is to provide an artificially safe place for clients.

Time and Temporality The impermanent nature of life is another inevitable attribute of the world that affects every single human being. Each of us is aware of the temporality of each action and of the transient nature of every interpersonal relationship. There is universality in that all human beings respond to these inevitabilities, although each one of us will act in his or her individual way.

Time is closely connected with ending, which usually evokes many emotions. In therapy this needs to be addressed as it is a vehicle for the clients' explorations of their world-view. In trying to keep boundaries in therapy, agreeing time and the sequences of the sessions are vital ingredients of the therapeutic framework. It is important to have a starting point and to refer back, when needed, to this commitment. I believe that the nature of any existentially oriented therapy involves awareness of time.

The difference between open-ended and time-limited therapies lies in the fact that the time-limitation and the ending provide a different working character to therapy. In time-limited therapy, the time limitation provides both a positive and negative attribute to the therapy. The positive side is the intensive nature of the encounter. The negative aspect is the therapist's tendency to be taken over by the client's desire for a 'quick fix'. This in itself may impede the therapeutic process. Therapists could become so involved in their own desire to cure the client that in the process they could, paradoxically, become counterproductive. They need to be permanently vigilant in this type of therapy, and suspend this tendency.

Ernesto Spinelli has argued that the therapist's strong desire to cure the client gets in the way of the therapy (1994). As a compromise, we introduced the modular system in time-limited therapy (1997). This means that the contract always incorporates the possibility of further therapy modules. For example, if the agreement is for twelve sessions and one or two review sessions, the contract will stipulate that, should the necessity arise to introduce other modules, this can be negotiated.

Although the intensity of the (initial) therapy will be compromised, our experience shows that the pressure of time and temporality remains a major factor in the 'mood' of the therapy. The ending of the therapy is always linked with pain, loss, and memories of separation. The concept of ending and the temporal nature of the therapy are in some respects therapeutic tools and need to emerge often from the background to the foreground of the therapy.

Interpersonal Relationship One other given of being is that we create interpersonal relationships in response to the insecurities and the temporality of the world. We can also say that the moment we are born we are with others and that we are relating to each other. Our basic concern as human beings is to express ourselves to others, which is a precondition of living.

We create an environment in therapy that is conducive for clients to express themselves freely. Interventions in therapy can produce many types of outcome. The less active type of intervention will create conditions of calm and an empathic, trusting environment. Clients may feel freer to express their innermost feelings, including hidden shame, and each niche of their existence. To do this, we create, in the words of one of my clients 'a bubble in a vacuum'; this means an empathic, trusting relationship where clients may explore and reveal their innermost emotions and their perceptual mind.

In divergence from this, it is also important to facilitate clients to discover their ambivalences, and to challenge these. It is necessary sometimes to tune out of our total identification with clients and view them, and our relationship with them, from a wider perspective. Hence, I challenge my clients at times rather more purposefully, but always empathetically and encouragingly. This can take many forms such as rephrasing clients' statements by making them simple and clear. Body language or just gentle intervention can be enough. This may make clients aware of the possibility, not only that they can also observe situations from different perspective, but also that those changes are feasible. In a way, this process moves the client from passive to more active thinking.

Value and Sedimentation Human beings, cultures and families create values. These are sometimes spiritual, moral, or other behaviour codes. These values provide meaning and serve to create different types of strategies for living. They instigate positive or negative emotions, according to our ability to fulfil or frustrate our goals.

'Sediment' may be described as 'the matter that settles at the bottom of a liquid, but by continuous stirring, we can move it. Some values can become very rigid; these may be called rigidly sedimented. Sedimentations can sometimes be positive but when they become too rigid, they may also cause problems in life. Yet, sedimentation can in theory always be shifted ...' (Spinelli: 1989), even though sometimes it takes longer and a great deal of effort.

When we speak of values, the story starts when we as human beings lost our innocence – by moving from an unaware to an aware being – and our guiltlessness. Through our consciousness we were able to value good and bad. Our prehistoric hunter predecessors were permanently subject to the threat of annihilation by other predators, natural disasters, hunger, and diseases. Somehow, they had to acquire a good system of values, strategies and a variety of skills, in order to remain alive, individually and in groups. The most important manifestation of this was the search for security which our distant ancestors sought in the shape of food and shelter.

Today, we are in an eternal quest for security. Or, to put it differently, we are seeking to move from insecurity to security. When we analyse our present Western, cultural, family and ethical values, we cannot escape from this fact. Given that our principal values are spiritual, we find security in the values in which we invested meaning. The same applies to all values, material, interpersonal, or artistic; they all provide us with security. By realising our values, we feel secure; by failing to live up to them, we become frustrated and insecure.

Some of these values can be so strongly embedded in our character that we cannot imagine being without them. Values which are so strongly and rigidly stuck in our constitution that we cannot even contemplate being able to shake them off, we call 'rigid sedimentations'. Such sedimentations always awake emotions.

Polarities The creation of values means the creation of polarities. If we say that something is good, this presupposes that something must be less good or no good, namely bad. Polarities are very important in my own world-view and I prompt clients to explore their own polarities. For example, a client might feel that the only way to exist in the world is by modesty. The polarity of modesty is showing off, which itself can be positive or negative depending on our attitude, context, and circumstances of events. Polarities are complementary to each other and not necessarily antagonistic.

Aspiration and Meaning The psychiatrist Victor Frankl, a survivor of the Holocaust, developed his existential theory called Logo Therapy on the premise that meaning is a vital tool for human survival. His experience in the camps has shown that people who encapsulated meaning in their life – whether spiritual, ideological or simply finding meaning in telling the story of the Holocaust – had a better chance of survival (1988). Frankl's own meaning in life, as he described it, was to propagate the need to create meanings in life.

My own experience of therapy is that when clients lose their meaning, depression ensues. Meaning is interconnected with our values, our aspirations, and our strategies for survival. It is, therefore, one of the tools with which clients recognise their own world-views. Whilst each individual develops meaning, values and aspirations in their own way, no one can escape the process of developing meaning. Everyone is influenced by cultural and family influences, but each of us can add or subtract from these influences so that we can live an authentic life based on our own assumptions.

Meaning and aspiration are very much connected with our self-esteem. In fact, we develop our aspirations in order to maintain our self-esteem. Some people need to gain power and control in order to maintain their self-esteem and security. Some need to become a Napoleon or an Alexander the Great. Others need to become wealthy, or write books, become a better artist, or a great scholar. Some immerse themselves in spirituality. There are in fact innumerable ways to find security and joy. The question that arises in therapy is to what degree the clients' rigidity is embedded in their value and behaviour system. Are they able to vary the degree of their aspiration and meaning to a more acceptable way of being?

It is important to realise that therapy is about degrees and not about absolutes. A client had difficulty in relating to people. He felt rejected, not listened to by most of his friends, and had special problems in relating to women. In therapy, it transpired that he felt embarrassed to ask questions because he believed that he ought to know everything. If he did not know something he expected immediate rejection and his self-esteem would plummet. As a strategy for survival, he developed a method of being an 'all knowing' person. Even in situations where he wanted to learn more about a subject, he was incapable of asking questions. Instead he made statements and waited in the hope that the subject would be clarified by discussion (Strasser/Strasser:1997).

Choices and Free Will Within the constraints and limitations of the world, all individuals can exert various choices. In fact, Jean-Paul Sartre argues that we are 'condemned to be free and must forever choose. He meant by that, whether we choose or not, we always make a choice. For Sartre, the very fact of being in the world is freedom of choice. Even if we do not choose, we have chosen (1958:632). This means that if we are unaware of a choice that has been made, it is still a choice. If I am not aware and did not choose to be late to my lecture, I have still chosen to be late.

In therapy, there are always an infinite number of possibilities to choose from, albeit within the limitations of givens in our lives. We can feel ashamed of being short or tall, but at least we have the choice to change our attitude towards it. One can, after all, accept it and be proud of it (Strasser/Strasser:1997).

The prospect of choosing is of great importance in therapy. When clients know how they function in respect of their issues, they will also become aware of elements of their world-view. They will then be able to make a choice on how to change and adjust their values and aspirations, and see how this will change their behaviour pattern.

The Self – Self-Concept The question of 'self' is a central issue in most psychotherapeutic models. There are many ways to describe the self. A person-centred therapist would describe the self as a 'core self' which would be actualised if the 'shoulds' and the 'oughts' which we acquire from our culture did not obstruct it. Fritz Perls (1959) believed in a constantly changing self, whilst Freud believed in the id, ego and super-ego construct of the self (1984). (A detailed discussion of this lies beyond the scope of this book.)

Our self or self-esteem fluctuates, depending on the situation we are in. If our aspirations are frustrated our self-esteem moves from a secure place to an insecure place – from a significant to an insignificant place. What we do to maintain our self-esteem depends partly on our world-view – what are our aspirations, meanings, values, and what is our attitude to changing some of those value systems.

Thus, the self has many aspects which also manifest themselves in emotions. Sometimes we are an angry self, sometimes we are a jealous, joyful or a sad self. Nevertheless, we can say that our real self is the conglomerate of all selves. We create our self-concept and self-esteem according to our value and belief systems. Our behaviour patterns are dependent on our values and self-esteem, but can also be sedimented.

The way we interpret the word 'self' influences the client's therapy. One of my clients complained that he felt uncomfortable in life because he could not be his 'real self'. He said that he would like to be the spontaneous self he had been in his youth. He had been outgoing, carefree and able to do the things he wanted. In his adult life, however, he felt constrained by his need for the constant approval of others. This he perceived as an inhibition to his 'freedom'. He felt that the only way he could be secure was to be that extrovert boy who had been unrestricted by any social or worldly limitations. In order to be happy, he had to regain his 'real self'.

His anger and fear were also aspects of his different self that were looking for security. In therapy, he recognised that his anxious desire to become his 'real self' was only one manifestation of one of the many aspects of himself. His quest for unified stable self was a futile exertion.

FURTHER CONSIDERATIONS IN THERAPEUTIC WORK

Empathy and Direction My own structure of being, i.e. how I exist in the world, helps me to empathise with the client. I observe my own bodily self and my perceived assumptions. Being aware of my own postural behaviour helps me to observe my client's body language. My training in Alexander technique and yoga makes me aware of my own breathing patterns, which in turn enables me to facilitate bracketing and suspend my assumptions. At the same time, this allows me to facilitate clients to see some of the discrepancies, contradictions, and ambivalence that comprise their world-view.

Empathy is the most important element of therapy. Without empathy there is no interpersonal relationship. To tune in to the client and to identify with their emotions is an art in itself. It is also important to have the capacity to tune out and facilitate the client to see their situation from a different perspective and challenge their ambivalences.

A lot of concern in the therapeutic community is about 'direction'. In existential therapy, we do not direct clients and tell them what to do. Rather, we follow their train of thoughts and emotions. We prompt them to reveal themselves. As opposed to giving advice, we believe that, by guiding clients, they will learn from their own experiences, and obtain insights. We agree with the humanist tenet that non-directive counselling is one of the most effective methods (Rogers, 1980).

Yet, we should be aware that complete non-directive counselling does not exist. The reason for this is that the moment that we have chosen to intervene, ask questions, answer back, we will have 'directed' the client and chosen a theme. The non-directive approach means for us, therefore, that we encourage clients to challenge and arrive at their own conclusion. We accept that our clients always know best.

Focusing This brings me to the notion of focusing on issues in therapy. It is not the aim of the existential approach to focus on particular issues, or to set specific targets or goals – as some cognitive behavioural and some brief-oriented therapists may do. I rely on my belief that all issues are linked. An advantage of working in this way is that I have the comfort of time, even in time-limited therapy. Generally, one issue will reveal and interconnect with all other issues.

Interaction of All Givens In ending this section, I would like to emphasise the importance of the fact that all structures consisting of various givens continually interrelate with each other and connect self-esteem in a totally non-linear and non-chronological order. What this means that any of the client's sedimented issues will reveal their respective world-view. Thus, I believe that I can support clients more directly and empathetically by following their disclosures.

INSIGHT

The degree of rigidity in clients' value systems and behaviour patterns will determine the time needed for clients to become aware of their world-view. This awareness in itself can change or shake clients' beliefs and value systems. Yet, in my experience, more often than not this produces the hoped for changes. The awareness of knowledge of one's world-view needs to be integrated in the client's total being.

There is a need for an empathic, trusting relationship in which this acquired knowledge may be reviewed repeatedly, and this should produce new insights. In the words of one of my clients 'I know, I know and I know that it will click, although it will be repeated and repeated'. For this, we need an environment that becomes the 'vacuum bubble' I referred to earlier.

CONCLUSION

The purpose of therapy is to create the conditions and environment in which clients can explore and reveal their world-view. Clients will be able to see their discrepancies and contradictions. These discoveries are usually not 'earth-shattering' revelations, merely revelations of what they already knew. This re-acquaintance with that which is known may produce insights which in turn create further insights, so that the known facts become 're-known' and 're-felt'.

Our structure of being and the awareness of how we therapists exist in the world – in other words the awareness of our world-view – provide us with a support to be empathet to the client and to be a therapist instead of doing therapy.

In this process, emotions play a vital part. Emotions are always present in all our actions. And they disclose the client's world-view. These emotional aspects cause clients to rediscover their value and behaviour systems and become aware of some of their rigid sedimentations.

At the same time clients will not only have the opportunity to challenge their value and behaviour patterns, but also to exercise their free will with reference to change. Admittedly, changes are at times constrained by the givens and limitations of the world. Nevertheless, when clients absorb the process of the therapy it enables them to deal with any issues during, between, and after the end of therapy. Issues will always emerge and reappear, but a client's knowledge of how to deal with them will remain. I have attempted to demonstrate this in the graph that appears on p. 166.

2

Emotions

Many philosophers, scientists and psychologists have laboured from pre-Socratic times onwards to find the right way to define the term emotion. Yet, no consensual definition has ever been found. The history of the search for an adequate theory is a frustrating one. There is a proliferation of theories of emotions, from philosophers such as Aristotle, Descartes and Hume, to psychologists such as Freud, Jung and Watson, to Darwinists, cognitive scientists and many others. Countless books and studies are available. In *The Psychology of Emotions* (1996) Richard Lazarus offers an overview of the entire spectrum of the main current theories, outlining the concepts of the different approaches.[1]

Emotions have been suppressed and have received a negative press since time immemorial: crimes and misdeeds have been committed because of uncontrolled emotions. For example, if we are angry and we do not suppress this anger, at some point, we will be capable of killing or injuring people. Yet, every emotion has its own function and can sometimes be regarded from a positive as well as from a negative angle. Only in this century have emotions been considered a holistic part of human existence.

At this point Aristotle's theory, expressed in the 'master and slave' metaphor, should be mentioned. His theory goes that emotion is a primitive, unintelligent, bestial human expression. Wisdom and reason must, therefore, be firmly in control, and dangerous impulses need to be suppressed. This notion of 'dangerous' emotions has had an enduring influence on Western Civilisation. Throughout the Middle Ages, Christian philosophy was preoccupied with a notion of sin caused by emotions. David Hume was one of the first philosophers to challenge the inferior place of emotions, though in saying 'Reason is and ought to be the slave of passions', ultimately, even he fell back on the Aristotelian model of master and slave (Robert Solomon, 1993:3).

Emotions in Therapy

The role of emotions in therapy cannot be over-emphasised. Every emotion is connected with the givens that illuminate our world-view. In fact, each emotion is a manifestation of an aspect of our world-view. Indeed, it could be said that emotions are the best tools for clients to re-discover and re-acquaint themselves with some aspects of their world-views and with their ambivalences which brought them to therapy in the first place.

So, what are emotions? James Hillman writes of 'a curious and over-whelming confusion ... a kind of scepticism about the possibility of theorising about emotion' (1961:5/7). I could not think of a better way to describe my own thoughts in investigating the theories on this subject. We can account for actual experiences which illuminate universal themes in the way we respond emotionally to the world. On the other hand, we can also account for the infinite different ways to experience emotions. This is what this chapter and the book is explores.

In his book *Emotion and Adaptation* (1991), Richard Lazarus presents a cluster analysis of no less than 135 emotions. There is an inherent difficulty in defining each emotion precisely and separately, not only because of the complex nature of emotions but also because each emotion is usually attached, linked, and interacting with other emotions. For instance, when I am angry about something I am also, depending on the circumstances, jealous, envious, hostile, bitter, hateful, or vindictive, and so on. One of the purposes of this book is to demonstrate how any emotion, on its own or in conjunction with other emotions, can help everyone explore and become aware of their world-view.

REFLECTIVE AND UNREFLECTIVE EMOTIONS

In therapy, it is important to distinguish between reflective and unre-flective emotions. When clients divulge their emotions, many of them remain in the background and may emerge in the therapy. Taking the example of anger again, most of the time we are unaware of anger itself. We only feel physiologically and psychologically that we are antagonistic towards something or somebody. The moment we have appraised and evaluated these emotions, however, we can speak about them and explore how have we experienced them.

My experience with clients shows that emotions express themselves in these two ways. There is a moment of expression that appears as an instantaneous, startling, non-aware, primary expression. This may be followed by an 'aware' experience. As soon as clients become aware of their emotional experience, they can evaluate it, explore it, and get away from that spontaneous feeling of being totally out of control. The former of these experiences I would call an unreflective and the latter a reflective response to emotions.

I derive these terms from Jean-Paul Sartre, who defined emotions by their unreflective state. According to Sartre, an emotion is only an emotion when the individual is not aware and not contemplating his feelings and actions. Sartre, at the age of 34, first expounded his theory of emotions in 1939 (published in English as *Sketch for a Theory of Emotions*, 1962). This work was in essence the precursor to his monumental existential work, *Being and Nothingness* (1958).

Although, I have found Sartre's ideas about emotions very much relevant to my work in therapy, in respect of his theory that emotion is always 'unreflective', my experience does not coincide with Sartre's thinking. My work with clients conveys the necessity of being conscious of both modes of emotions: those which clients are and are not aware of.

Sartre's belief about unreflective emotions rests on the notion that emotions can be maintained only if and when an unreflective immediate rapport between 'subject' and 'object' has taken place. For example, if I am attacked by a vicious animal my focus of attention is 'riveted to it'. Any contemplation and explanation of the situation would break the 'spell' of the terror. In an unreflective emotion, I am 'under a spell'; everything else lapses into the background.

It follows from this, according to Sartre, that as soon as we contemplate and evaluate our emotions they are not emotions anymore (1962). Sartre goes even further. He maintains that emotions transform the world into a magical place. When a revolver is held to my head, I am under a spell and will lose control and faint. I faint in order to annihilate the threat. According to Sartre, I transform the world by 'magic' into a safe place.

This argument works well for negative emotions such as fear, anger, disgust, and so on. When, however, we look at a positive emotion such as joy, it is difficult to see the existence of a spontaneous unreflective state. 'Joy' would appear to connote a harmonious contemplative state – a state of reflection – as it does not cause either trembling or fainting, for example.

Nevertheless, Sartre argued that a joyous individual behaves impatiently, because his or her desired object is not available as yet. For instance, if I am expecting someone who I love, but she is not yet there, I am frustrated. Thus the joy-emotion becomes a negative unreflective emotion and may be treated exactly in the same manner as anger or other negative emotions (1962).

Here, Sartre is criticised by, for example, Joseph Fell who argues that his analysis of joy is too contrived to suit his concept of emotion (Fell, 1965: a similar argument is put forward by Fell where Sartre, 1962, disputes that anguish is an emotion because it is a reflective cognitive state, the result of a reflective contemplation). Sartre's theory particularly suits negative emotions, but it is somewhat obscure when it comes to joy and other positive emotions.

Furthermore, assuming joy has a reflective state, this state appears to fall under Sartre's emotional incantation theory. According to Sartre, 'emotion transforms the world into a magical place', which suggests that this state of joy must be an emotion, as more than anything it is able to create such a spell.

It is worth noting here that some philosophers would say that emotion is only an emotion once we experience it: in other words, only once we have evaluated and interpreted it. This is the opposite view of Sartre's. Thus, for example, Michael Lewis proposes that 'Emotional experience is the interpretation and evaluation by individuals by their perceived emotional state of expression' (1993:226). We *have to become aware* of our emotions before we can say that we *experience* emotions. Lewis substantiates this by saying that a change in one's neurophysiological behaviour must take place before we can say that we experience emotions.

In this respect it is interesting that some neuroscientists' findings coincide with the view of reflective and unreflective put forward in this book. J.E. Le Doux from the University of New York, a well-known neuroscientist, has researched the pathways of the brain and illustrated how we evaluate our information and our emotions. Most psychologists and neuroscientists follow his findings which suggest that our brain is relaying on two neural pathways of information (1993). One, an automatic pathway leads through the amygdala, which is in words of Keith Oatley *et al.* 'the central emotional computer for the brain evaluating sensory input for its emotional significance' (1996:151). According to their research, primary receptors transmit information through this pathway to the amygdala. Emotions activated through this sub-cortical pathway result from rapid, minimal automatic evaluative processing. However, emotions that need to be cognitively appraised are relayed to the neocortex. Such a circuit is thought to be the basis for the appraisal and evaluation of events (1994).

EMOTIONS IN THERAPY

This description is remarkably similar to what we therapists see in therapy. We therapists often encounter clients who ask us to help them quell their outbursts of anger, guilt or similar emotions. What these clients appear to be asking is to be purged of these primary 'unreflective' emotions. Clients need to explore this desire and realise that with the best will in the world therapists cannot do away with this type of primary emotion. Unreflective emotions are part of the givens of our existence, though we do have the capacity not only to evaluate but also to stop ruminating about them once we are aware of them. In other words, reflective emotions are emotions we *can* control. Otherwise, if we were angry to the extreme, we would never be able to stop killing.

One of the aims of therapy is to explore both types of emotion. When unreflective emotions emerge into one's awareness, they can be examined and discussed, and clients can discover their ambiguities and challenge them. We might say that as soon as clients become aware of their emotions they are already in a reflective mode: clearly, one cannot explore something which one is not aware of. The process in therapy is, therefore, to facilitate the unreflective emotions to emerge into reflective ones.

One could rename reflective emotions as 'conscious' or 'aware' and thus come nearer to Sartre's idea of emotions always being in an unreflective mode. But for the intimate and sometimes highly charged atmosphere of therapeutic encounters, it does not matter how we name or how we argue about the semantic aspects of emotions. What matters is how we may prompt clients, in the most empathic manner, to explore the emotions which aquatint their existence and to call into awareness the unreflective emotions through which they can explore their world-view.

Jacob

A good example of this is Jacob, a mentally disabled person and the holder of a 'green card' (a detailed case study will follow in Chapter ten). I perceived him as a 'professor', because of his eloquent, concise and mainly ivory-towerish views. I have learned as much from him as from many learned books and philosophers.

In one of our sessions, I examined his anger and fear towards a black person. His instant anger and fear were inexplicable to him. He felt an intolerable hatred and physical and psychic aggression towards this person. As this feeling had repeatedly overcome him, he had become anxious about his own reactions. He was encouraged and prompted in therapy to evoke and express his hatred, and to become aware of it and explore it. The question was, what was he angry about?

It soon transpired that he perceived this person as a threat to his job and his existence. Jacob was subsequently able to connect this with his self-esteem. He became aware of the fact that the anger was a vehicle for him to maintain his self-concept and security. Then, after a considerable silence, he asked in a naïve fashion what the purpose of emotions was, arguing that his anger and hatred must have an aim. This in turn brought him to a spontaneous suggestion that the person he was angry with was a foreigner, and that this created an unfamiliar, threatening situation for him. He was protecting his self-esteem and his existence. At that moment he felt guilty and compared his racism to that expressed by others against Jews. Feeling especially guilty he muttered: 'How can I as a Jew tolerate this instinctive dislike of another race'.

WE ARE NEVER WITHOUT EMOTIONS

It can be seen from this that emotions can bring about positive as well as harmful experiences. Emotion usually starts with an unreflective, unaware sensation and when it becomes a reflective, aware sensation we can control it. In therapy, the capacity to observe and to listen to clients' emotions is the most important part of the therapeutic process.

I find that emotions are always present in every single activity or manifestation in therapy. I often have clients who experience difficulties in identifying and getting in touch with their emotions. Yet, emotions are continually embedded in human consciousness. They are always available for exploration in therapy, even when clients say they are searching for them. Their aspiration to get in touch with their emotions itself includes a strong emotion. This can be a strong desire, a passion, or a fear of not succeeding in their aspiration.

2. Emotions

From a theoretical point of view, for Sartre, too, the fact that emotion is always present in our consciousness is a revelation of one's consciousness. Mary Warnock quotes Husserl in the introduction to Sartre's *Sketch for a Theory of Emotions*: 'Emotion is precisely consciousness'. If this assumption is true, then it is also applicable to every aspect of therapeutic encounters and a client saying 'I cannot get in touch with my emotions' is for him profoundly challengeable.

Most psychologists and theorists have come to a similar conclusion. For example, Carroll Izard, an eminent biosocial evolutionary scientist, arrived at this conclusion from a different theoretical viewpoint. He writes: 'Always emotions: we are never without feeling' (1991:80). His thesis is that emotions are constantly with us and that they play a very significant role in how we interpret the world around us.

Louise

The case of Louise, an ex-client, exemplifies these considerations. Her case was characterised by the problem that she was incapable of expressing her sexuality. This she attributed to her inability to access her emotions. In therapy, she stubbornly held on to her belief that if only she would discover her feelings her problems could be solved. She had tried numerous types of therapies, which had only confirmed her goal. She felt that she was a person who could never achieve this, and so she put all the blame for all her trouble on this inability. If only she could discover how to get in touch, at the deepest level, with her feelings, this would instantly cure her 'appalling and shameful' feelings about her sexuality.

In one session, Louise became resentful towards me and asked me in an irritated way why I did not focus on these deep feelings. I asked her to stay with this irritation and this was followed by a long silence. I urged her to explore it, how it felt to be in this irritated state. Louise became even more irritated with me because she felt that she was losing control. She then explored her feelings about losing control. Louise realised that she was 'in touch' with her emotions and that her problem was not the absence of emotion. On the contrary, her emotional life was very active, but it was directed at controlling the revelation of her shame. This was the beginning of an insight that enabled her to work on her shame and other issues.

EMOTIONS INVARIABLY HAVE A MEANING

This assumption is another lynch pin of existential therapy. When a client shows an emotion, it is always directed at something. Jealous, envious, angry clients are ceaselessly manifesting their emotionality against something or somebody. To put it differently, emotions are the best vehicles for clients to disclose themselves and reveal their world-view. Disclosure of emotions unveils to the therapist what they are angry about, and what their frustration or joy is about. This, in turn, illuminates the clients' values and their sedimentations and it leads them directly to a position where they can challenge their rigid sedimentations. Furthermore, emotion always discloses an individual's self-esteem. Therapists who listen in order to prompt clients to express their emotions will be able to help clients reveal some aspects of their world-view and to challenge it.

I will illustrate this from my own experience. Recently, I experienced an extremely moving situation with a close friend. The pain my friend was feeling touched me deeply and I wept. Next day, a relative of mine asked in a way that felt like an accusation why I had wept. I was totally unprepared for this and I just felt 'thunderstruck'. I cannot say how long this sensation lasted but, when I started to analyse my feelings, I acknowledged a momentary hostility, anger, vengefulness and resentment towards someone I love. Instantly, I knew that these vehement emotions towards a person who is near to me must stem from my own issues. It dawned on me that, like every emotional impact, this was very much connected to my self-esteem.

By further analysing the situation, I realised that the residue of a rigid sedimented value, saying that a man should not weep, was still with me. Thus, I became aware that my hostile emotions were a protection against the threat of being belittled and ashamed. The anger put me for a moment in a more secure and superior place than feeling like a helpless small boy who had wept. Through this analysis I became aware of one of my early values – that I could only be accepted by others and myself as a worthy person through being strong and emotionless. I realised that I could also have considered weeping as a strength rather than a weakness and an important aspect of my world-view had been disclosed.

Sartre's main assumption is that emotion is always present in our consciousness and that emotion always means something. He took the latter notion from Husserl, who put forward the notion of intentionality, meaning that our consciousness is always intentional with regard to something. From this, Sartre developed the doctrine that emotions like all mental acts are directed towards something, an object. The word 'intentionality' originates from the Latin root *intendere*, meaning to stretch forward. Spinelli describes it as the vital propensity of our consciousness and quotes Husserl 'Consciousness is always consciousness of some thing' (1989:11). Each emotion has intentionality to direct itself at something. When I am worried, I am worried about something. When I am angry it is always in relation to somebody: I am emotional about my frustration that somebody has not fulfilled my expectations.

Uniqueness and Sameness

Emotions not only reveal an individual's world-view, but also disclose the diversity of each individual. We all respond to the givens of our existence. In the fact that we all do this lies our sameness. Our differences lie in how we react through our creations of values and behaviour. We all manifest and experience our emotions, but we all differ in how we experience them and react to them. Furthermore, emotions and behaviour patterns differ not only between individuals, but also within each individual to varying degrees.

It is quite remarkable to observe the changes of the intensity of clients' emotions at different times. For example, in one session, Cherry expressed her immense pain in getting up in the morning to face total meaninglessness because of her perception that she had large buttocks.

I felt that the session had become very intense, and that her sadness and other emotions affected her deeply. I felt her pain and I thought that I identified with it. I felt that I intervened empathetically in reflecting back her pain. But I also challenged her to explore other meanings in her life.

Cherry became vexed and warned me: 'You are exactly the same as everybody else. You cannot understand my real pain'. I then realised that I would never be able to reach the depth of her pain; her perception was different to mine. Tomorrow the same pain would probably be different to today's and so would her feelings. Subsequently, we explored this and Cherry was quite taken aback when I told her that I could never understand and identify myself one hundred per cent with her emotions. After this, I felt that the trust between us augmented and that my observation had validated me in her eyes.

WE CONSTANTLY REVEAL OUR SELVES

As mentioned earlier, whether we are aware of it or not, we do disclose ourselves through our emotions. Warnock refers to Heidegger and writes: 'in emotion ... we can rediscover the whole of the human reality, for emotion is the human reality assuming itself and emotionally-directing itself towards the world' (1962:25). In this way, Warnock and Sartre propose that through intentionality of our consciousness and through emotions we constantly reveal ourselves. In therapy, therefore, the therapist's capacity and skill to listen and recognise emotion plays a vital role in helping clients disclose and recognise their world-view.

Although John had no therapy with me, his behaviour in an exploratory session exemplifies how emotions can reveal in some aspects of individuals' world-view. He telephoned for an appointment and we agreed the time, date, and fee for this exploratory session. This meeting was to enable us to get acquainted and to see if we could work together. The house where I practise is difficult to find, so I gave him very precise details how to get there. At the time of the appointment, two o'clock in the afternoon, there was no sign of John. Twenty minutes later, the telephone rang and a very angry and impatient voice said: 'Where is your house, what are you doing to me – I have been driving round in circles for an hour.' I explained again as patiently and as precisely as I could, how to find the house. A further ten minutes later John shouted on the telephone: 'I should be at my office, or I should be at home, rather than sitting in a car for an hour or more.' After yet another telephone call John arrived in a fury. I guided him into the consulting room, while in an irritated tone he said that had he known how difficult it was to find me he would have not come.

It took a few minutes for John to calm down. I asked him whether he wanted to talk to me about any problems, so that we could see if we were suited to work together. In an agitated tone, he delivered a monologue about the fact that he could not understand his wife and two daughters. His daughters had totally abandoned him and hardly wanted to speak to him. 'I have given them everything that life can offer, luxury, a good education and they have never wanted for anything. I cannot understand why my wife wants to divorce me. When I try to speak to my children they are curt and disinterested in what I have to say.' I prompted him for a concrete example. 'When I last spoke to my daughter in California on the telephone, she barely listened to me. I became justifiably angry. I told her what I thought of her, after which she had the insolence to hang up'. After further prompting, he explained that his temper always rose quickly when he felt certain that he was right. He could not tolerate people who would not listen to his views which he knew were sound. John explained that he had built up his career and life by hard work and that he provided for his family with everything they could ever need. I encouraged him to speak about his work. He explained that people treated him in a similar manner to his family. He gave them everything, but they did not appreciate his generosity.

We were nearing the end of the session and I intervened and tentatively summarised as follows: 'John, what I heard was that when you think you are right and are not being appreciated you get into a temper.' He interrupted 'I know I have difficulty in listening but I only lose my temper when I am certain I am right.' I said to him that I did not doubt that he was right and kept his family in luxury. I also explained that what I heard was as follows: When he 'knew' that he was right but did not receive the expected response, he felt that he was in an insecure place. This provoked his anger and when angry, he could not appreciate his family's needs and vulnerabilities. I stressed that this was what I gathered from his account, but I also asked him to correct me if I misunderstood something or some part of it. His reply was that while he heard what I said, he was still right. After all he gave them everything they required, but they still rejected him.

I told him that I was sorry the session time was over, but that I felt that we could work together. I asked him whether he could work with me. He then produced a list of a large number of professional therapists, some of whom practised much nearer to him. He said it was impossible for him to travel such a long way to find my house. I patiently went through the list and referred him to a therapist who lived near him. He got up and headed towards the door just as I asked about my fee. He asked 'How much?' I explained that it was the same as agreed over the telephone. His instant answer was to ask for a reduction because of the difficulties in finding my place. I told him that I could not give him this. As he started to argue his point, I said I would rather he did not pay at all. He then tried to justify himself.

I told him if he ever needed any help in the future to call me and wished him good luck with the new therapist. He left without paying me.

John revealed many aspects of his value system. One of his important beliefs was characterised by his view that through money and material advantage he was entitled to everything, from family love to every single other aspect of life, including happiness. He also believed that when he was right he was justified in losing his temper and exercising power to get his way. His behaviour pattern was very much dependent on what he perceived was right or wrong. Overall, material success provided the overwhelming meaning in John's life. Through this he maintained his self-esteem and found a secure place in this world. In the course of this process, he completely disregarded his family and others as people. This he manifestly demonstrated by a behaviour pattern of disregarding the needs of others.

It can be seen from the above that emotions give away and disclose many aspects of an individual's value and behaviour systems. In the above case, emotion was mainly anger with other associated emotions. These emotions not only disclosed how he appraised his world in terms of his values, but also what his strategies were for maintaining these values and behaviour patterns. Moreover, as stated before, these behaviour patterns were needed in order to defend his self-esteem. The graph on page 167 exemplifies the way in which all the givens, including emotions, interconnect.

NOTE

1. Another of his books (1991) describes his psychological adaptive theory of anxiety in detail, an investigation based on cognition, motivation, social, and abnormal psychology. Carroll Izard classifies and describes anxiety from an evolutionary, developmental and biosocial perspective (1991). The humanistic existential psychologist and psychotherapist Rollo May, devotes an entire volume examining anxiety from an existential humanistic viewpoint (1977).

3

Anger

My own earliest recollection of anger is related to my German governess who reprimanded me for touching my genitals. She forced me to wear a girl's dress for punishment. Even today, I cannot imagine a punishment that provoked a more violent emotion in me as a boy. I shouted, screamed, and came close to destroying everything around me. I yelled for help. But nobody came to my rescue. It still remains an enigma to me how this could have happened in a home where love, care, and enlightenment were the ethos of the family. Both my parents admired German culture. We children had to learn German from an early age and the German governess was given carte blanche concerning our education. It is an irony of life that it was exactly this idolised culture which practically destroyed our Jewish family. Other than my sister, a cousin, an uncle, and myself, no family members survived.

Deterred by the governess's threats, I soon learned to restrain my shouting and screaming. She threatened to tie me to a table leg if I would not curb my rage. It is not difficult to imagine how lonely and abandoned I felt as a five-year old boy. Feeling like a total outsider, I was constantly the subject of her ridicule. She called me 'Zorn Pinkel'. For me this meant an angry midget – a worthless being. I perceived myself as being in an insecure and inferior position. My childhood was a long battle where I had to fend for myself 'to be a man' and prevent myself from falling into a bottomless pit of inferiority and insecurity. I felt that I had to 'toughen' myself to face the world. I worried that it might be discovered that I was treated like a girl. A large part of my self-esteem hinged on being accepted as a 'man' and my behaviour patterns were designed to protect this image. In my perception, crying was for girls and I made great efforts to subdue my 'weakness'. I had to be resolute and always aware of what I wanted, but I also had to be perceived as such by others.

35

Only after realising that my self-esteem hinged on acting like a 'man', have I been able to evaluate and challenge my behaviour patterns. The moment I became aware of the instantaneous anger related to the issue of 'manhood', I could appraise my behaviour and had the choice to reflect whether my self-esteem needed to depend on ' being a man' or whether I could identify other meanings in my life. I could explore my world-view.[1]

Approaches to Anger

In popular thought it is assumed that anger, rage, fury, etc. are all emotional reactions which indicate extreme displeasure. This echoes Aristotle's 'master and slave' principle according to which civilised people ought to control anger. However, some psychologists argue that anger should not be controlled, but expressed. They contend that venting anger in a 'catharsis' is a beneficial therapeutic tool. Fritz Perls's clients were encouraged to discharge their emotions both physically and verbally. Clients were prompted to exaggerate their aggression in a therapeutic environment by, for example, throwing cushions and hitting the table until a catharsis occurred (1959).

However, my experience with clients shows that, while awareness of one's emotions is part and parcel of therapy, prolonged rumination on it can become counterproductive. Venting anger uncontrollably in catharsis is misguided, though sometimes a spontaneous, angry expression can be useful. Indeed, assertiveness is a very important part of therapy to be explored. The function of the therapist is not merely to facilitate the awareness of anger, but also to promote the exploration of the benefits and harmful effects of excessive anger.

How , then, should anger be dealt with? On the internet someone wrote: 'Anger! The Hidden Killer! The repressed anger is a leading killer of love, joy, health, happiness, loving relationships, family, harmony, success and prosperity ... a killer of everything that we inherently desire ... everything that is good, lovely and fair' (1999). According to this view, the only thing to do is to get rid of this blight. Would that be useful? Is anger really such a vice?

Let me return to one of my own experiences to explore these questions. My late father was the eldest of five siblings. His father was a hard-working local teacher who pushed him to be educated, in spite of the fact that there was no money to support him. He had to support himself. From secondary school to graduation he earned his keep through tutoring and clerical work. As a result of his strong will and his effort, he managed to become a high-powered lawyer and barrister. Hence, our family ethos was influenced by his conviction that one should have high aspirations in life and that these can be achieved by sheer will. I clearly remember the day when I came home from school having failed my French exam. I knew that I would not be punished, but that my failure would cause grief to my parents. My father did not reprimand me, but he was visibly struck by the bad news and his mood turned sombre. He then tenderly took my hand and we walked up the hill to the vineyards, which surrounded the town where we lived. Climbing up the hill, he told me about his youth. I was impressed but also sad to hear him talk. He spoke to me about working at night to earn some money to feed himself and also about his enjoyment and on occasions when he could afford to go to a bistro and order a half portion of his favourite goulash. Then he told me: 'Remember that there is one thing that will help you in your life: you must have the will. If you will it, you will achieve it.' It was very well meant, though I may have misunderstood him. I willed everything in my life very hard. As a result, I achieved considerable things.

Yet, more often than not I failed to achieve my goals, which made me angry, at first, and then guilty that I had not willed it enough. Sometimes my anger turned into rage, first against others and then against myself. On occasion, when I was rejected by a woman or had failed an exam or failed to impress others with my ideas, I instantly became angry. Needless to say, this anger was also associated with envy, jealousy and other emotions, depending on the situation.

Now, is this anger of mine bad? The moment I recognise my anger I can also appraise the situation. Is it sensible for me to expect that I just have 'to will something' in order to reach a state of permanent security, irrespective of the limitations of the world? Is it right that all my self-esteem should hinge on that one sentence: 'If I will I must achieve'. If I do not achieve, must I use anger to feel more secure and more superior?

Having contemplated these negative aspects of anger, I also need to consider the wisdom of my late father's words. Where would I be without my strong will? A great deal of what I have achieved in my life, I can attribute to his words.

Is anger a vice or a virtue? My answer is: for me it sometimes is a virtue and sometimes a vice.

AMELIA

Background

Amelia was in her early thirties. She lived with her partner and two children, Daphne who was then three years old and Jason who was one. She had a brother who was two years her junior. Her family were all professionals: her father was a retired G.P., her mother a retired teacher and her brother a consultant physician. Amelia herself was a journalist and her partner was a lawyer. She appeared to come from a caring family background, although she could recall certain experiences from her early school days that indicated that she had suffered some setbacks that had affected her self-concept. In therapy it soon became clear that professional and intellectual endeavour constituted a very important part of her value pattern.

Therapy

At the end of a term, I met Amelia in the college cafeteria, where she introduced herself as a journalist. She wanted to know more about existential time-limited therapy and asked if she could have therapy with me. I enquired whether her desire to have therapy was only to gain some experience in the existential approach, or was it for her own needs. Amelia replied that she felt that she needed some support in her life.

We had a lengthy discussion during which I explained to her that, although I also took clients for open-ended therapy, most of my work was based on a modular time-limited model. I explained my views on the differences between time-limited and open-ended therapies, and we agreed that we would look for a suitable time to begin therapy. Since I did not have a vacancy at the time, we decided to meet again in three months. We would at that point determine the mode of therapy and detail the contract between us. I did not take any notes other than her telephone number, just marking the time and date in my diary.

In October, Amelia arrived at my consulting room, very punctually. She gave me the impression that she was a serious person who was trying hard to downplay her charm and good looks. She was of average height, yet she appeared, by slouching, to minimise her stature. As much as I wanted to suspend my judgement, I could not help but note that, even if Amelia herself was unaware of it, she fervently wished to hide her real personality. Yet it was immediately clear that she was intelligent and easy to communicate with. Despite these considerations and her frequently manifested timidity, I did not feel that her issues would be of such a nature that twelve sessions and the usual two review sessions would not provide the desired results.

The 'Presenting' Problem

As Amelia began to present her problem, I queried her expectations and anticipation of the effectiveness of the therapy. I also cautioned her that before we made a final agreement we had to explore whether we would be compatible in therapy.

She unfolded her story slowly and articulately. She lived with her partner Henry, who was the father of her two children. As she spoke, she slumped and looked down. It appeared to me as if she felt heavily burdened with carrying the world's woes. From time to time, she glanced up at me and when our eyes met, there was always a slight glimmer of an optimistic smile. I felt that her stories, and the feelings she conveyed, were somewhat less distressing than her postural bearing suggested.

Amelia defined an uncontrollable anger as her problem. She frequently experienced this in her daily life and she found it intolerable. It troubled her deeply that even the most insignificant problem could trigger such a release of emotions. I prompted her to give me an actual example. She spoke of a recent experience. She was quietly and deeply engrossed in her thoughts while queuing somewhere. Out of the blue, a man pushed her aside to take her place in line. In a split second, she found herself in such an uncontrollable rage that she could have annihilated this man on the spot. When I asked her to explore this phenomenon, she associated this anger with a similar emotion to the one directed towards Daphne. For no apparent logical reason a bout of anger against him would regularly erupt, about which she would feel both guilty and ashamed.

I now felt that it was time for us to discuss and define the framework of the therapy. We clarified Amelia's expectations of the therapy and we completed our contract. We settled on twelve sessions, one per week, plus two review sessions. Should the need arise, we could always negotiate a further module. We also agreed on confidentiality, commitment, fee, and dates. As it transpired later, I forgot to discuss the length of each session.

The Story

In subsequent sessions little prompting was needed for Amelia to tell her story, to challenge her own contradictions and to become aware of her world-view.

My intention here is to relate some of Amelia's experiences which were relevant to her understanding of her world-view. This understanding, I believed, was also of critical importance in her life. It was necessary to clarify them further in therapy, and relate it to her 'presenting' problem.

Amelia was brought up in a very close-knit family whose members were intellectuals and held liberal views. She complained that she had few recollections of her early childhood. Yet, she clearly remembered that at an early age she felt excluded from her peers and that she felt different from the other children in her playgroup. She was ridiculed, mocked, and labelled an 'ugly Jewish girl'. I encouraged her to tell and possibly re-experience one of those instances. My motivation was to elicit from Amelia, in the present, the pain that she so feared. This, in turn, could open the door for her to examine her values and world-view.

In this incident, she not only experienced rejection, she also developed a feeling of being an 'outsider' to her peer group. The pain and despair was in the present. Indeed, she was convinced that she was different from her own age group, and in the back of her mind she harboured the idea that she really was this 'ugly Jewish girl'. Thus she argued that she would never be an 'ordinary' child or an 'ordinary' person, and would never be accepted in any respected group. This feeling of worthlessness and inferiority accompanied her through her life and into our sessions.

Self-Concept

In our sessions, Amelia attempted to examine her anger from all angles, how it felt, and what the anger was about. She explored how she felt when she was pushed aside, or was disregarded as a person. She managed to recall many of her agonising experiences when she was rejected, not only by her peers, but also, on some occasions, by her mother and father. She could often recall in the sessions her anguish and sorrow when she entered her primary school and was ostracised by her peers.

I felt her pain as if it was my own. My feelings of anger and the fear of my humiliating punishment came back to me. I was pleased in a way to have been able to identify and totally empathise with her sufferings, because through this I was able to appreciate Amelia's feelings. Yet, I knew that, as much as I wanted to empathise and was able to tune in to her experiences, there was still a gap between my appraisal of her feelings and her own perceptions. I knew that it was also necessary to distance myself from her problems. This was important in order to enable me to observe her ambivalence and to assist Amelia with challenging her own viewpoints, their contradictions and discrepancies.

Sedimented Value and Behaviour Patterns – Strategies for Survival

What kind of strategies of survival did she employ to avoid and escape from this painful feeling of isolation? We were by now both aware that anger manifested itself to Amelia as a symptom of a perceived threat of rejection. Anger signalled her fear of re-experiencing those feelings of uncertainty and inferiority that went hand in hand with loneliness and isolation. It did not take Amelia long to challenge herself and to become aware that her anger and the subsequent feeling of aggression helped her to dispel her feeling of helplessness, insecurity and inferiority. Amelia continued to narrate her story. This story was, however, already coloured with her awareness and realisation of at least part of her world-view.

To feel that she was a person of consequence and to maintain her self-respect, she had to be the best student and the perfect journalist. The fact that, even in the smallest task, in fact in each and every endeavour, she needed to be perfect didn't make achieving this easy for her. Her fear and anger manifested itself prominently when she found herself in an academic surrounding. Despite her scholastic background, she felt inadequate and had difficulty in engaging in an argument or a conversation. This elicited not only anger towards herself and others, but also envy of those who could mingle easily with people. Her low self-esteem was perpetually present. She could not discharge her emotions and she occasionally withdrew into a state of isolation. She harboured the fear that she would be found out, and that they would see through to her 'ugly Jewish' and inadequate self. From the very beginning of her education the quest for knowledge was her guiding motive. While success would give her the joy of self-approval, the slightest frustration would cause her long-term devastation. All her perceptions of failure were inevitably accompanied by the phenomenon of anger or withdrawal. The anger may have been directed toward herself or someone else. Emotions such as envy and guilt were interlaced with anger.

I prompted her to challenge her habit of attributing negative values to each and every experience. It appeared to me as though she had a compulsion to carry the whole world's pain (Weltschmerz) on her shoulders. In this respect we examined her body posture, her frequent slouching and her occasional avoidance of eye contact. She felt that her habitual bad posture as well as her occasional neck ache were in some way part of the sedimentation of her world-view. As her psychological behaviour pattern had sedimented and rigidified, so her postural pattern had also become a powerful habit. All revealed the same phenomenon.

I challenged her to also consider the positive sides of her life and her achievements. And as we worked together, she became aware of her rigid sedimented value pattern and her assumption that it was essential for her always to be perfect. Amelia realised that her rigid behaviour pattern prevented her from appreciating her positive sides, yet also that, in spite of these 'negative attributes', she was also motivated, ambitious and had obtained a first class academic education; she had two children who if not perfect, were certainly loving. She had developed an impressive personality, and in general she functioned well. She knew that she paid a price for all this in that she had difficulty in developing relationships, which she considered a weakness. On the other hand, she had the strength and wisdom to realise that she needed to work on her problems if her life was to change.

We reached a midway point in the therapy. Amelia arrived eight minutes late for a session, which was unusual as she had always been very punctual. She looked worried and seemed to be in a contemplative mood. She apologised for being late. She wanted to explore further her anger and the low self-esteem that haunted her. Without any apparent relevance to these intentions, she spoke of an episode with her father who taught her that she should never accept any authority's opinion without challenging it, and that she must be 'sceptical and open-minded'. She felt that she had integrated these qualities. Her statement provided the steppingstone from which I could issue the challenge, how was it that with all her scepticism she could not challenge some of her sedimentation?

Then, suddenly, she asked me how I felt about our last session, when we ran over time. I replied by asking her to expand on this question. She emphasised that she felt comfortable with it, even though boundaries were very important for her. From her reading she knew that time boundaries are vital in therapy. 'Are you angry with me about it?' I asked. She replied that she was not. I reminded her that she had said that boundaries are very important in therapy, so how was it that she was not angry with me? I asked by how many minutes had we overrun the present session? She said she did not know, because we had not specified the duration for each session at the first meeting. 'Then you must be doubly angry with me' I said. 'As you say this, I feel that I am a little uneasy' she answered.

Subsequently, we further explored our relationship. She came to the conclusion that she would be very reluctant to criticise me. She speculated that the reason for this could be that I would be hurt. Under no circumstances would she want to cause discomfort to me. To my question 'What would my anger do to you?', she replied that a rejection from me would drive her into the low self-esteem that she was desperately trying to fend off. She would not risk that for the sake of the boundaries.

What followed was a complete examination of her interpretation of boundaries, particularly those which concerned our relationship. We discussed the necessity of boundaries. She was surprised and concluded that the main objective of keeping a firm time-frame was to maintain an 'artificial' security for clients, for them to feel safe between the four walls of the consulting room. When I asked her whether the overrunning of the hour made her insecure she answered that she felt safe and appreciated. We both smiled.

I asked her whether the fear of trespassing textbook boundaries and challenging my authority were somehow connected. Did they both have to be perfect? She remained silent. Then exactly sixty minutes past the beginning of the session, I asked her what would she like to do: to stop or to continue the session for a few minutes? She answered, 'I don't know. What would you like to do?' Knowing that I had already overran the time for the session, I disclosed my own feelings and said 'I would like to stay silent for one minute, if you feel that you would like to do so as well'. She said that she would.

After a minute we both stood up and she murmured, 'this was a most ...' I could not hear or decipher her last words. In that last minute of silence I felt empathy with her, and I believe that she felt my empathy. On the whole I thought we had had a good and fruitful session. I hoped that she had experienced a number of significant insights, and that she would experience more of these insights between the sessions. I also felt that her world-view had become clearer to both of us.

Yet as is often the case after sessions like this, I experienced a niggling feeling. What if I was completely wrong in my intuitive assumption? This self-doubt has occurred many times in my life. The next session would reveal the truth.

At the next meeting, Amelia did not refer to the previous session. Instead, she spoke of her lack of 'social skills'. Her parents, her brother, and her partner were all well versed in communication skills. She was the only one who felt lost in an environment where she thought that she needed to 'perform'. She would rather retreat to a corner and talk with another individual than mix with the crowd. She sometimes felt angry and envious towards those who could socialise with ease.

Amelia recalled an incident involving Daphne, her three-year-old daughter. She was deeply absorbed in work on her computer, while Rachel constantly interrupted her. After persistent intrusions, Amelia lost her temper, shouted at Rachel, and had difficulty in restraining herself from striking the child. The threat of rejection of her work on the computer provoked her anger, which she directed at her daughter, and this in turn affected her self-esteem.

During our session Amelia complained of neck ache. She herself challenged her postural stance and her own reluctance to deal with this pain. She would not see a doctor or consider alternative therapy. Unfortunately, this session came to an end before there was time to reflect on Amelia's body posture in connection with her values and behaviour patterns. I had, however, made a mental note that when the opportunity arose, this question should be addressed.

I felt already at this stage of the therapy that Amelia had connected her compulsive behaviour pattern and value systems to her self-esteem. Her anger and associated emotional experiences were danger signals. They were patterns of behaviour in a struggle to become a more secure and better person, to be superior and to avoid her feeling of low self-esteem. The metaphor for her low self-esteem was that 'ugly Jewish girl', whose school experience was that of exclusion from her peer group. She understood that in order to gain approval, she employed a strategy of striving to be the best student, the best raconteur, mother, and wife. While she accepted the positive side of these behaviour patterns, she also became aware of the threat that under-achievement posed to her self-esteem. These patterns sometimes prevented her from relating to others openly and intimately. When she experienced the slightest rejection or frustration she would become emotionally charged, aggressive, or withdrawn. These conditions served to protect her self-esteem.

I felt that Amelia was fully aware of her desire to modify her value system and make her own choices. She knew that if she could only accept that she did not need to be either the best conversationalist or the best in her academic endeavours. She just needed to be content with herself. I was also convinced that in the remaining sessions Amelia would need less intervention from me for her to counsel and challenge herself.

Insights

Despite the fact that in most situations Amelia was able to clarify her ambivalences, her sedimentation and her low self-esteem, her compulsive behaviour pattern still persisted. She recalled an occasion, when she knew in advance that her self-esteem would sink, yet she felt unable to alter her actions. Nevertheless, some slight transformation had occurred in her position, primarily as a change in her *approach* to her self-esteem. She could predict what would happen and could connect her self-esteem with her value system. What is more, she could challenge herself by considering what would be the worst that could happen if others did reject her: would she really feel insignificant? She admitted that while she could not control her behaviour and her low self-esteem, the consequences of those aspects of herself, for example her depression, had not lasted for as long as usual. So, Amelia gained some insight with which her life, albeit almost imperceptibly, had changed.

In the eighth session Amelia was irritated. Much as she challenged herself, reminding herself that she was well-educated, a good journalist, and in the main good looking, she still lacked self-confidence. I listened as she challenged her view that she could purge herself entirely of her low self-esteem. She argued with herself that if she could only accept her periodic feelings of low self-esteem she might not need to fight to such an extent to protect herself.

On her own, she explored what it was that made her so angry when, against her wishes, her partner Henry took a ten-minute nap. She realised that if she felt disregarded as a human being by him, then she felt abandoned and thus insecure. The words 'ugly Jewish girl' crept into her mind and for a moment the anger that was generated made her feel superior. I asked her whether she felt that in an ideal world she would never feel inferior or unsafe. Amelia stayed with this question and came to the conclusion that if she never felt depressed, she could never feel the opposite, nor could she appreciate approval.

Although she accepted this, she was still bothered by the degree and frequency of her mood swings. She then spoke of her lack of regular sexual contact with Henry and was irritated by her own lack of libido since Jason's birth. Amelia also felt uncomfortable about the fact that all her previous affairs had lasted five years and that she was the one who had initiated the separations. Indeed, her partnership with Henry was rapidly approaching the fifth year. Another separation would prove her inadequacy. During this session she challenged her own lack of consideration for Henry and her desire and difficulty in acknowledging a less then perfect solution. She found it problematic to accept or contemplate that her own postnatal condition could be the reason for her temporary lack of libido.

Although we had, from the early stages of the therapy, discussed the importance of the element of time in therapy and its inevitable ending, on this occasion I asked Amelia how she would feel if for some unforeseen reason, this would be our last session. If so, I prompted her to discuss what had been her expectations of the therapy; what kind of positive or negative effects would she take away with her from our work together? Amelia was quite taken aback by this, as she was hoping for another ten-week module. She was, however, able to list positive aspects that she would take away from the therapy. We concluded that the primary one was that, in her opinion, she had absorbed the process of therapy, and that she would be able to deal with her issues independently.

From this session on, I tried to intervene less, giving Amelia the opportunity during sessions to challenge herself. I was only there with her, with empathy, supporting her in her exploration. During the tenth session we spoke about the ending, and she expressed her feeling that she was uncomfortable with the thought of concluding therapy. In subsequent sessions we discussed what ending would mean to her, and again whether she could deal with her own issues. This session and the final one were used for reassessment of our expectations, to discuss how Amelia felt between sessions about the therapy and how she foresaw herself subsequent to our parting. We then discussed another module on the basis of a new contract and new boundaries. In this new set-up I proposed that the second module would be based on my written recollections, and how I perceived our therapy. Amelia would then read it and comment on it. I had also told her that I believed this experience could be rewarding for both of us. She felt flattered with the proposal and agreed to go ahead with this in the next module.

After a considerable break we started our second module. Without any introduction, she brought up an incident regarding her partner. When he had come home she had been angry with him for not acknowledging all her hard work during the day, caring for the children, amongst other things. He insisted on talking about his business, paying little attention to her. She had managed to provoke him into anger. In this session, Amelia eagerly explored the reasons for Henry's and her constant anger. I decided not to intervene, as I wanted Amelia to work independently on this issue. The only intervention I made was to link her previous love affairs with her relationship with Henry.

She spoke again of her inability to maintain relationships for no longer than five years. After five years she usually lost her libido, and found another partner. However, things were different this time. Although her relationship with Henry was approaching the critical fifth year, she argued that they had a continuing commitment to each other, and to their children. Furthermore, her loss of libido might be a consequence of her postnatal state. The implied question and debate was, would they be able to survive the critical five-year cycle?

Amelia wondered whether the source of Henry's permanent anger could have been her consistent refusal to have sex, which may have provoked his deep and sometimes hidden frustration. Her behaviour would, at least in part, explain his anger, or so she argued. On the other hand, her own loss of libido seemed partly time-related. During this whole session, Amelia continuously explored the similarities between her relationship with Henry and her other relationships. She began to understand Henry's anger and her own anger with herself, being over-burdened with work, children and feeling disregarded as a person by Henry. She realised, in a deeply emotional way, how Henry felt when she ignored him, and when she rejected his sexual approaches. She felt that, while her own low self-esteem was a source of her anger, her responses must have evoked emotions in Henry to protect his own security and self-esteem.

These thoughts followed a philosophical discussion between us about the idea that during the period of anger, or associated emotions, we are incapable of appreciating the vulnerabilities of others. I knew in my heart that Amelia was entirely capable of continuing her own self-explorations. Furthermore, I was also convinced that the following sessions could assuredly be based on Amanda's own analysis and her own comments on her case notes.

Amelia's Self-Therapy

I allowed Amelia to read part of her case notes. She agreed with my perception of her in general, but started to analyse my notes further. 'Yes', she said, 'even though my present lack of libido maybe due to my postnatal state, I still think that my five-year cycle needs further exploration'.

She explained that her relationship with sex was sometimes completely detached and 'objective'. In this mood, she regarded herself as an observer and saw sex as a 'futile, purposeless, grotesque exercise'. In discussing this issue, I reminded her of her early experience with her father when he taught her that one of the most important qualities in life was scepticism. This session was then marked by her investigation of her sceptical approach to the sexual act. Was scepticism for her a positive or a negative experience?

AMELIA'S COMMENTS

Anger

I am still angry. Yet, soon after the event, I am now able to reappraise the emotional incidence. My behaviour pattern consisted not only of expressing anger, but also of ruminating and holding grudges. Now, I am aware that my anger does not only reveal the threat of rejection and that of insecurity, but also many aspects of my world-view. I am conscious that my first defence strategy is anger and is sometimes appropriate; just the knowledge of this gives me the opportunity to change my attitude towards my behaviour.

3. Anger

I still express my anger spontaneously, but soon after the event I can let go of it altogether – both when it happens with my partner and my children.

Insecurity

In therapy, I became aware that anger served my need to escape feeling inferior by attempting to make myself feel superior. Freddie prompted me to explore the connection of moving from a feeling of insecurity to security with my self-esteem. This made a great deal of sense to me. It also allowed me to feel less punishing towards myself for my impulses.

In therapy, all these feelings of insecurity were connected with my behaviour of withdrawing from social situations. While this still prevails and I find myself from time to time feeling less confident in social situations, I now strive to accept that this is the way I am and not see it as a problem that I am not the centre of things or able to hold people's attention. Understanding the urge to quit insecurity for security made me better able to tolerate insecurity.

Mediocrity

Freddie allowed me to see how much of the time I was talking about my need to be perfect and this led me to fully grasp something that I had only been intellectually aware of – that if I wasn't perfect I was somehow a failure. He asked what my feelings were about the word 'mediocrity' and I had to admit that I found the idea of the word being applied to me unbearable. It made me think about what would be so bad about not being 'special' – as I saw it. As mentioned, I still get angry but, while I am enraged, find myself able to consider what it might be like not to be angry.

CONCLUSION

I strongly believe that before deciding on, or accepting, the conditions of therapy, clients should get a taste of what will follow. I find that during the first session it is beneficial to explore and discover as much as possible about the client's world-view. Conversely clients should gain knowledge of the therapeutic process.

This, I feel, serves dual aims. On the one hand, the more I understand the client, the easier it is to prompt them to disclose themselves and to become aware of their ambivalences and discrepancies. On the other hand, during this process of prompting disclosure and extolling clients to challenge themselves, it appears that they are able to clarify and evaluate the process of therapy. They should have the opportunity to accept or reject the therapist. Indeed, during our first session, I felt that Amelia revealed at least part of her world-view, although only vaguely, through her behaviour pattern, body language, emotions, and the content of her story. This I noted, without disclosing my thoughts. I anticipated, however, that in therapy Amelia would soon be able to unfold the issues that relate to this.

Amelia's case shows how it was possible for an intelligent individual to grasp her own world-view in a very short time. She was, then, able to challenge herself about her rigid sedimentation and compulsive behaviour patterns. Amelia explored and linked her frequent anger to her value system. When, in her view, she was not performing to her high standard, she either became angry or withdrawn. These values were so embedded that she had to be the perfect scholar and the perfect raconteur. Any threat would take away her self-confidence. She needed this protection.

Amelia did not instantly achieve her aim to totally change the compulsive nature of her anger and her withdrawal patterns. She could not abandon them even after recognition of her sedimented behaviour. Namely, anger was that which made her secure and superior.

Nevertheless, awareness of these aspects of her being had initiated an insight of self which somewhat altered the quality of the emotions and the consequences of her behaviour pattern. I believe that by exploring her problems, Amelia had gained new views that would in turn trigger further insights.

I also feel that Amelia recognised that there would always be some new issues to explore. Indeed, it can be seen that Amelia worked on her own explorations and pondered her own ambiguities in the second module. In my mind I considered the second module as a 'life rehearsal' for her post-therapy life. It was most interesting how her positive evaluation of scepticism revealed some of her world-view. While scepticism helped her in many aspects of her life, both intellectually and generally, it also prevented her from experiencing appropriate interpersonal relationships. Her scepticism about close relationships at times inhibited intimacy, as did her sceptical attitude towards sexual relations. Now she realised that although a sceptical attitude could serve her well on occasions, it could also distance her from intimate human relationship.

Amelia's world-view in each of her emotional states is symbolised in Graph B at the back of the book. For example, when she had a row with Henry, this was triggered by her feeling his disregard for her. Amelia fell into her insecure state, which was connected, as can be seen on the graph, with the uncertainties of the world. This is what she experienced at that moment. As a response to this insecurity, Amelia became furious, which in turn put her into a more secure, or rather a superior, frame of mind. As a result, Henry now felt insecure and inferior. He now became angry and began to shout at Amelia in order to regain his own feelings of security and superiority.

After some time both of them started to laugh spontaneously about these outbursts. Amelia realised that her aim to achieve perfection for her sedimented values and have a consummately 'perfect' relationship with Henry motivated her to move from insecurity to security. Yet, she also knew that she possessed the free will to choose to surrender control and laugh at the whole incident.

NOTE

1. Nonetheless, sometimes one may be entirely unaware of anger. Recently somebody told me 'You are angry'. My immediate reaction was: 'Not at all – you are angry'. It took me quite a while to appraise my emotional state. This is a typical example of interaction between unreflective and reflective emotion mentioned above. The unreflective anger was my involuntary primary unaware reaction, while the evaluation of the process was the reflective anger.

4

Fear and Anxiety

When I personally think of fear and anxiety, I cannot get away from the following scene. It happened sometime in October 1944. I lived in Budapest, under Nazi occupation, with false identity papers. I used to visit my sister and my brother-in-law, who also had false documents, in Buda, which is part of Budapest. One day my sister discovered that her neighbour was an old school friend of mine who had become an ardent Nazi. From time to time, his wife came for a chat with my sister and my visits to her flat, therefore, had to be carefully planned. On one occasion, within half an hour of my arrival, the doorbell rang. At my sister's urging I just managed to hide under her bed in time. It must be remembered that at the time thousands of naked Jews were marched to the Danube to be shot. I probably spent no more than thirty five minutes under the bed, but in my perception it seemed an eternity.

My feelings about those thirty five minutes are the crux of this story. They began with a certain bravado: 'I am in a superior position; I can hear this Nazi, but she cannot see me'. This feeling of heroism gradually disappeared and turned into dread at the fear of being discovered and tortured before dying. Finally, I became paralysed with fear, but very conscious of every second passing by. It was the fear of annihilation. My body was frozen, but I could still think. Even now, I can still vividly remember the thoughts of those 'last' minutes. Any death would have been preferable to the humiliation of Nazi torture and punishment. I recall thinking: 'If only I could escape from this terrifying situation every moment of my life will be a joy'. Eventually the woman left the flat. Clearly, a few months after the end of the war life proceeded as normal, without that 'permanent joy'.

The episode has remained with me all my life and serves as a memento in times of distress or despair. Often in my life, when I have felt insecure and my self-esteem has begun to ebb, those mental images reappear to help me view situations from a wider perspective. When I reflect on this episode, and I contemplate the values of cowardice as opposed to heroics, I feel that I was lucky to have had the determination to save my life by being a 'coward'.

Anxiety and Fear

Conventional thinking about emotions distinguishes between anxiety and fear. Fear is an emotion that is evoked by a recognisable external threat, whereas anxiety is provoked internally. There is also a distinction between the normal as opposed to the neurotic and the existential anxiety. Rollo May best describes the difference between the normal and the neurotic anxieties in *The Meaning of Anxiety* (1977). He postulates that normal anxiety is a reaction that is not disproportionate to an objective threat and 'can be relieved if the objective situation is altered' (209). Neurotic anxiety is the reverse: 'it is a reaction to threat which is ... disproportionate to the objective danger' (214), and cannot, therefore, be relieved by the altered situation.

Existential anxiety, on the other hand is a universal phenomenon. It is our deep-seated response to the uncertainty of life and to the temporal nature of our existence. While this anxiety is always lurking in the back of our minds, it need not necessarily be negative. The knowledge of our death, and facing our transient existence, can provide us with a true taste of life – a more vibrant and intense life. In Yalom's words 'death is the condition that makes it possible for us to live life in an authentic fashion' (1980).

In the above experience, I felt no difference between fear, normal, neurotic or other anxieties and other emotions. I just feared, dreaded, felt anxious about the threat to my being and envious of others who were not in my situation, who were 'free'. These emotions were interlinked with many other physical manifestations – numbness, trembling, a lump in my throat, and other symptoms.

Anxiety and Fear in Therapy

Individual emotions of fear and anxiety are difficult to distinguish from one another. In my experience, they have therefore no relevance in therapy. On the following pages, when Barbara, one of my clients, revealed her fear of disclosing her vulnerability about her accent and her working-class background, there was no observable difference between anxiety, fear, or other feelings; there was just a bundle of mixed emotions. What was important, however, was that Barbara was able to reveal through her emotional experience her low self-esteem and her values. In other words, she was able to unveil part of her world-view.

This kind of fear and anxiety does not, however, negate my own and my clients' experiences of so-called existential anxiety: a constant apprehension about the inconsistency and the uncertainty of life. This existential anxiety is compounded by the perpetual, yet frequently repressed knowledge of our impermanence and our temporal existence in this. Existential death anxiety, aloneness, and isolation go hand in hand. To perceive our temporality means that we understand we are finite that we must all die. In the final analysis, this is one journey we have to travel alone.

The fact of our certain ending also limits our choices in life. This, however is not a morbid view. On the contrary, our death gives significance to our lives. The recognition of this should provide us with zest for life and with a source of creativity. From this standpoint, death is not regarded negatively. Grasping the awareness of our finite existence may provide us with a more intensive and authentic approach and may also give joyous gravity to living (Strasser/Strasser:1997).

This existential anxiety is not a peripheral threat that may be separated from other sensations. Even at their most basic level, everyday questions hold a degree of natural anxiety. And this is what we explore in therapy, namely how we can fruitfully go about our daily lives, knowing our limitations. Existential anxiety is of real significance in our work with clients. Anxiety which is intrinsically connected with the uncertainties, limitations and temporal nature of our life, is a fundamental constituent of our being in this world. In therapy, clients frequently wish to eliminate all obstacles and anxieties, which they experience in life and in therapy. Some of these anxieties are connected with the temporal nature of our whole existence, and clients need to accept the transient and temporal nature of all life experiences in their relationships, not least in therapeutic encounters.

BARBARA

Background

Barbara, an elegant mature woman, came to me for therapy. She was extremely well-spoken and highly articulate. She came from a working-class background, her father was a taxi driver and her mother a housewife. She had begun disassociating herself from her 'hostile' background at an early age. With sheer persistence and willpower, she got into a grammar school. Most children at her school were upper-middle class. They resented and bullied Barbara because of her accent and background. In spite of this, Barbara finished her schooling with good results. She then embarked on a career that eventually took her to Milan where she worked as a fashion buyer. There she had a few fleeting affairs, followed by one that lasted several years. When that relationship ended, she returned to work in London. Some time later Barbara had met Howard, a widower with two teenage sons, who eventually became her husband. Ten years into her marriage, she gave up her job in the fashion world and decided that she wanted to study music. As her interest in music waned, she went into therapy for four years while she read social sciences. Again, she dropped both, completing neither the therapy nor her music studies.

Therapy.

When Barbara entered my consulting room for our introductory session, I showed her the way and pointed to two armchairs. She chose the one near the window, which she used right throughout the therapy. At the introductory session, I prompted Barbara to tell her story and relate her problems. I reminded her that the first session was simply for us to become acquainted and to examine whether we could work with each other. She began to present her problems and told me of her difficulty in communicating in social situations, which she had come to dread. As the story unfolded, it became clear that she was well versed in her own explorations but was much influenced by theories. She spoke fluently and concisely; making sure that what she said would be logical and understandable. Her focus on pronunciation and her lucid style were remarkable. She and Howard, her now retired physician husband, were engaged in an active social life. They entertained a great deal. Despite her wide social experience, Barbara felt deep trepidation not only while preparing for these events, but even more during the occasions themselves. She felt that all her husband's professional colleagues and friends would look down on her. She assumed that her 'cultured' accent was all too transparent and that they would detect her working-class background and would despise her for it.

She then asked me where we would go from there. I explained that as far as I was concerned, I could work with her. I pressed her to ask any questions before finalising the therapeutic contract. I explained that if we worked together, I would be there for her to express and reveal all her feelings and emotions and those issues that she had not expressed elsewhere. I would assist her and guide her to discover some of her ambivalences and would help her to become aware of discrepancies and doubts in her belief and behaviour systems. Thus, she would explore her daily life and how she related to the world. This might enable her to challenge her own values and behaviour patterns and bring about some desirable changes in her life. To enter into this relationship would involve serious commitment from both sides. I stressed the importance of time in our sessions and explained the modular approach to her. I clarified that, should she want to work with me, we would have to agree in detail on the therapeutic framework.

Barbara listened attentively and without hesitation agreed to work with me. I suggested that she should not make an immediate decision. She should reflect upon it and telephone me when ready. We discussed all conditions in advance and agreed on fees and confidentiality. However, we argued about the suggested time limitations. After four years in therapy, Barbara had considerable difficulty in accepting the concept of a time limit. Following our discussion we agreed to ten sessions followed by two review sessions, with a promise to look at further modules if need be, though the essence of the therapy was to bear in mind the limitations of time.

Next day she telephoned me and accepted the contract. As she arrived, I asked 'How are you?' before she sat down. Barbara was surprised at the question, as she had not been accustomed to exchanging everyday pleasantries with her previous therapist. 'Why did you ask?', Barbara wondered aloud. In my practice, I use the time between entering the room and sitting down to exchange ordinary niceties in order to make the session more relaxed and congenial. This I call the pre-therapeutic buffer zone.

We soon discovered that the motivation for her enquiry was to find out what kind of therapist I was. I evidently did not conform to her perceptions to the 'rules' of psychotherapy. We searched deeper into the question whether she could utilise our sessions for her benefit, even if I was not a good therapist. 'How are you?' as a question, was explored further. We examined if such a mundane inquiry, in her perception, could be to the advantage or the detriment of her therapy. Barbara soon realised that her views on therapy were very much conditioned by certain rigid assumptions. She judged each situation with her knowledge of psychological theories, acquired from reading, and from her previous therapy.

From the start of the therapy, I tried to prompt Barbara to express her emotions, including her feelings of shame, in order to throw light on her world-view. Put simply, what were the values that evoked such deep responses? Barbara's presenting problem revolved around a compulsive behaviour pattern. This revealed itself in her feeling of being intimidated when meeting people. Repeatedly, she regarded friends she met as intellectually superior. As these emotional experiences were all too frequent in her life, she sought help to overcome this in therapy and find her 'real self'.

Presenting Problem: Fear of Being 'Found Out'

Without any preamble Barbara began to talk about her experiences with Robert, the man she had lived with in Milan for several years. She described him as a well-educated Englishman from an upper middle-class family. Although she loved him and they were happy together, she was haunted by her fear of inadequacy. She dreaded Robert's family finding out 'everything' about her, which would elicit social and personal rejection.

I encouraged her to investigate further what this 'everything' was. What was it that she so dreaded to reveal? I asked her what would have happened if Robert had found out about some of those perceived shortcomings. She replied: 'If for instance, he had known how little I valued myself, I believe that he would not have valued me either and would have left me.

'You separated in any event, Barbara', I remarked. 'Yes, but he was not the one to leave, I was', she said. Barbara had been attractive in her twenties. However, at the time, she not only lacked life experience but also 'schooling' in social skills. Her good looks helped her to attract and relate to men. Yet, the slightest hint of disapproval threw her back into an abyss of despair. Her perception of herself as a person with low social status and inadequate education was deeply ingrained in her.

I urged her to examine in the present, what the fear of this rejection and the rejection itself would do to her. It was not difficult for her to recall and to re-establish the fear and the anxiety of the isolation and loneliness. I empathised with her pain, as I could feel her rejection through my own issues. I asked her where else she had experienced feelings of fear, loneliness, and rejection. She described how, when she was young, her ailing grandmother had come to live with her parents. From then on, as Barbara perceived it, her grandmother monopolised her mother's attention. Since Barbara regarded her father's presence as a threat, she felt totally dependent on her mother. Yet, in her eyes, her mother had neglected her. She felt completely abandoned and a sense of worthlessness dominated her. This was the kind of feeling she experienced frequently throughout out her life. It had cast a shadow over all her relationships, especially those with Robert and now with Howard. She described her daily struggle to keep at bay the feelings of insecurity and worthlessness which accompanied her in all aspects of her life. I reflected how this talented woman could put such negative connotations on her behaviour pattern, which, after all, had helped her to become an intelligent, well-spoken and cultured woman.

I urged her to challenge herself positively. After some prompting, Barbara acknowledged that she had personal strengths. Her low self-esteem and her behaviour pattern had had a valid function. They had been the motivation for working hard in order to improve and educate her. The fact that she had had the will and the ambition to remove herself from her predicament was a sign of real strength, although she had paid a price for it in her difficulty relating to people. She began to accept that her whole life was coloured by the fear of 'discovery'. She had to fight and in some way escape from this pitfall. She needed to find a strategy to avoid the feelings of uncertainty and worthlessness.

We explored her low self-esteem in greater depth. In one of the sessions during the therapy, Barbara fell into a highly emotional state: 'Why do I have to feel afraid of being rejected every time I meet other people. Where does this feeling of shame and self-contempt start and finish', she wondered. I pondered what self-contempt meant for Barbara. We both knew that her strategy for survival was based on withdrawal from people whenever she perceived a threat to her self-esteem. What did this deep feeling of self-contempt mean to her? What was the pay-off? Was her self-contempt preferable to rejection and humiliation by others? Was this contempt a strategy to hide, to distance herself, from the greater pain of rejection?

In one of the sessions, I found myself in a moment of spontaneous intervention. I said quite clearly and directly: 'Your problem is not your low self-esteem, but your belief that you are the only person in the world to experience it and be ashamed of it'. This intervention was totally out of character with my normal way of working and I was taken aback for a moment. Normally my interventions are focused on the client's own explorations and conclusions. I would have preferred it if Barbara could have looked at this issue without direct prompting and then have arrived at the same conclusion.

I felt that Barbara was shaken by my intervention. She asked me if it meant that others, including me, sometimes felt that way. I let her explore whether even people who had been given a lot of help in childhood experienced pain and rejection in their adult relationships. I thought that at that moment she gained a true insight.

Barbara remembered well a painful incident at grammar school. A group of girls were talking about spending a few days in one of their homes. Barbara asked if she could join them, but she was told there was no room. As she walked away, she heard one of the girls say: 'Who does she think she is?' I felt this remark was symptomatic of Barbara's view of life. In every situation where she felt uncomfortable, an inner voice asked 'Who do you think you are?'

Spontaneity

In one of the following sessions, I prompted Barbara to examine the issue of spontaneity and to explore situations in which she was content and happy. She described memories of being a happy and confident young child before her grandmother had moved in. In particular she treasured the memory of not being concerned about what people thought of her and said that she longed to be that happy child again. 'Could you enlarge on that?', I asked, 'What does being a happy child really mean to you?'.

'I would like to recapture the spontaneity and confidence of the little girl that I was', she said. Barbara then remembered an incident: 'I recall going to a friend's birthday party when I was five years old. I 'threw' myself into the games being played. I forgot all about my loneliness at home, I forgot about everything and I can still remember how much I enjoyed myself.' Barbara wanted to be an adult, who would be unaware of adult knowledge of the uncertainties, pitfalls, obstacles and inconsistencies of the real world and simply act spontaneously. 'I feel that what you are missing is the spontaneity experienced at that moment and lost since', I suggested. I also thought that this incident fitted in with her longing for a mother's unreserved love.

All this had a strong impact on me. I considered whether the remaining few sessions would be sufficient for Barbara to find her own way to further insights. As it happened, we negotiated a second module.

The Dream

Barbara found herself in a large cluttered attic in her grandmother's house, looking for something, though she did not know what it was. What she found was a Russian doll, the kind that opens to reveal other, smaller dolls inside. Exploring the meaning of the dream, Barbara felt that the doll was a symbol of her search for her 'real' self. The doll became a topic in our subsequent sessions as we reached the end of the therapy module. The sessions were characterised by the two images: the doll and 'who do think you are'. We were looking for that spontaneous little girl, who was not bothered how others would perceive her.

The nearness of the end of the therapy made Barbara somewhat restless. She became quite irritated with me about my 'power' to limit the number of sessions. I felt pleased with this particular emotion, as it was the first time she had shown any dissatisfaction with me and had expressed it clearly. I encouraged Barbara to express every aspect of her anger. She concluded that she was envious of her friend who had been in open-ended therapy for the past three years. I prompted her to hypothesise how she would feel if, due to unforeseen circumstances, I suddenly died, so that there would be no more therapy sessions. I felt touched by her protestations of sorrow. Despite the hypothesis, we were able to continue and explore further the positive and negative aspects of the therapy.

I was impressed with her capacity to see her own world-view and with the way, she was prepared to deal with her own issues. From that session onwards, I felt I only had to be there to facilitate her with the minimum of intervention. Indeed, she challenged herself hard and I felt that she was now ready to work on her own. We could therefore finalise the course of therapy after the two review sessions. Barbara disagreed with me as she felt she needed more support. In one of the last sessions, we agreed to continue with a new module of twelve sessions, but only after a considerable gap.

Second Module

Barbara arrived exactly on time, as usual, for the start of the new module. We began to work on the issue of 'what it is that is so difficult to disclose and why'. In the process of her intense 'internal dialogue' she tried to understand what it was that prevented her from feeling free to be herself. Could this be connected with her contempt of herself? She debated whether she was ashamed of her low self-esteem or of something more deeply rooted within her. She then spoke of a dream.

Second Dream

'I am playing the piano in the middle of a large, empty room. Suddenly I cannot remember the rest of the piece and I panic. I look up and I see the menacing figure of my father standing silently in the corner. My mother is observing me from a distance'. Even in the dream she knew that her father never approved of any of her achievements. Indeed he always reprimanded her by saying she should do much better. I felt that although this dream was short it was very rich in emotions. I thought that it would be meaningful for Barbara to capture the significance of these emotions.

I asked her later if she could describe her feelings in the dream. She paused and said 'I felt fear, trepidation, hopelessness and anger'. I prompted her further to interpret the dream and she began to talk about her father. When she was a child, he would humiliate her with sarcastic remarks and when he did this in front of other people she felt deeply ashamed. Her father's cruel wit, together with what she perceived as the loss of her mother's affection, left Barbara feeling abandoned and unloved. Thus, she was also injured in her capacity to love herself and so fell into the feeling of pain and despair that sometimes still engulfed her. I empathised with her feelings of pain and despair. Not only did I feel her anger but also that her emotions were justified. Yet, I tuned out so that I could view the situation from an objective standpoint. I asked Barbara to put herself, in the dream, in her father's position and to explore his emotions. It did not take Barbara long to understand her father's vulnerability. He had come from an abusive family and she realised that his wounding remarks came from his own deep-seated weaknesses and helplessness.

Barbara continued to analyse her dream. She felt her mother's anger against herself in the dream, but she felt that this was only a reflection of her father's emotion. Father made mother submissive, forcing her to comply with his wishes to be angry with Barbara. When I asked Barbara to imagine her mother's feelings in the dream, she became aware of her mother's anger towards her father for making her submissive. It was no surprise to me that in pursuing this further; Barbara began to see her mother's vulnerability and her underlying love towards Barbara.

Barbara explored her deep shame that underlay all the other 'shames'. She hypothesised that if her parents rejected her and believed that she was worthless, she could not accept herself as a worthwhile individual. It seemed to me that this dream illuminated for Barbara her emotions of the fear of disclosure.

Paradoxical Intention

In a later session, we explored the possibility of paradoxical intention. This is when the client is encouraged to do the very things she fears. This is used in the 'Logo Therapy' described by Victor Frankl in *The Will to Meaning* (1969). Barbara referred to a recent lunch with one of her husband's former colleagues and his wife. Her need to be liked and approved of had made her so anxious that she was over-effusive and had said 'all the wrong things'. This was for Barbara another rejection and yet another 'failure'. I empathised with her. I do not usually use paradoxical intention as an intervention. Yet, somehow, I debated this within myself and did exactly this. 'Could you explore what happens when you next meet them, behaving as if you did not want them to like you', I asked her. Barbara laughed and said: 'If only I could'. Yet I had the impression she was taken aback. Perhaps for the first time, she saw the real possibility of being able to change the way she related to people.

As we came to the end of the session, I made a very short intervention, asking Barbara how she felt at that particular moment. 'I feel free to be myself', she replied, 'because with you I feel secure'. 'Can we celebrate this now', I asked. She smiled and we noticed the sunshine on the veranda. I then asked her: 'Do you feel free in the sunshine, looking at this wonderful view? Can you stay with this?'

During the last minutes of the session, I asked her 'What prevents you from feeling free with others if you can be free here?' Her reply was 'Because I am confident that you accept me. You still treat me with respect even though I have told you about all the things I am ashamed of. With other people, I assume that they would reject me if they knew all about me'. 'So, that means that if you could only accept yourself you would not feel so threatened by other people's opinions', I responded.

I felt that Barbara was now ready to challenge her ambivalence. Could she feel free with others to the extent that she could with me? She already knew that in this therapeutic setting she was accepted as a valuable person with all her self-imposed negative values. Her working-class background, her unfinished studies, her shame of her shame, were all revealed and accepted.

New Possibilities

The following sessions were mostly spent on Barbara's explorations of various possibilities in developing new meaning in her life. She considered going back to her music studies. When I questioned her about her interest in music, she reluctantly admitted to being able to play the piano 'by ear'. I pointed out the sheepish way she told me this and we discussed how difficult it was for her to say anything positive. I felt that she was pre-empting the possibility, that I might dismiss her talent (as her father had done) by dismissing it herself.

I knew that Barbara's expectations of the therapy were not unrealistic. She understood that her cognitive appraisal of her world-view, and the challenging of her discrepancies, would not produce an immediate release from her 'shackles'. She knew that she would need to continue this exploration on her own in order to gain further insight. While she understood the meaning of the negative connotations of her values, she also had the capacity to challenge herself and examine the positive side of those rigid meaning systems that provided her with the strength and ambition to achieve the things in her life she could now be proud of. I also believed that by now she could challenge her wish to find her core self, her child-like real self. She realised that her inner-self constituted many aspects of her being.

Epilogue

At our last meeting when all the ending discussion and reciprocal feedback had been completed, a strange desire to disclose my own experiences overwhelmed me. I am always very careful with the revelation of my own problems. I always teach and warn supervisees to be reticent with disclosures and to consider whether they do it for they own sake or for the benefit of the client. Hence, I pondered till the last minute of the last session and then said: 'I must tell you about some recent experiences that made me identify even more with your problem. After all, "Who do you think you are?" followed you right through in your life'. I then told her my story of humiliation by an eminent cardiologist, which resulted in my own version of 'Who do you think you are' in daring to meddle in medical sciences.

By a strange turn of fate, the event took place before my renewed contact with her. When we met, Barbara consented to write her own comments down for publication. I had recently changed GPs. My new GP suggested that although I had had a heart murmur since birth, I should now have my heart valves checked. This was to be a routine precaution. I was somewhat reluctant, but still agreed, as my last heart examination had been five years ago. My condition was symptomless, and my quality of life as good as ever. I was therefore fairly relaxed when my cardiologist informed me that one of my heart valves was causing the murmur. He suggested that I should have a further angio-echogram in a few months, to monitor possible deterioration.

After the second echogram, my cardiologist pronounced that immediate heart surgery was needed. He sent me to see a heart surgeon as a matter of the utmost urgency. As I mentioned, my heart condition was symptomless. I was fit, and I had always been involved in demanding sports. I, therefore, decided to investigate my condition in general medical literature and on the Internet in order to obtain a second opinion. In my search, and quite by coincidence, I contacted a cardiologist from the world-renowned Mayo Clinic in the U.S. They asked me to send them all the relevant data. A great many e-mail messages were exchanged and they gave me as much information as possible. Any further comment, they said, could be only be given if they could examine me. They did, however, make it clear that there was certainly no urgency in the matter. As far as the fee was concerned, the eminent U.S. cardiologist replied instantly that there were no fees to be settled. 'I am paid by the Mayo Clinic, but please do ask any further questions that you may have'.

In my quest for the 'truth', I went for a second and even a third opinion. It was thus, at 8.30 am one day, that I found myself in an opulent waiting room of a well-known cardiologist. There were some ten fellow 'sufferers', who waited perhaps more patiently than me. After forty five minutes, I told the receptionist I had to leave as I had to give a lecture. Within five minutes, I was sitting in the consultant's room, answering his questions. He was both jovial and charming. I then said that I was questioning his previous diagnosis. I explained that not only had I researched my case in various publications, I had also used the internet to look for answers. There was a palpable change in atmosphere in the room and his tone altered instantly. In an authoritative voice he now asked me, how could I use the internet for such a delicate subject. How could I trust such a medium? 'If I really want to be treated, I must have trust in him and the surgeon'.

I started to feel as if I was sinking deeper and deeper into my chair, as if I was a boy trying to penetrate a 'castle' of science. This little boy did not have the right to meddle in such exalted matters or have sufficient understanding of them. It took the consultant less than five minutes to look at the test results, which he had not seen before. He said in a solemn voice: 'The pressure in one of your heart valves is five times higher then mine'. He asked me how I could doubt having an operation. How could I go to the US for advice, as they do anything and everything for money. 'Who do you think you are Freddie', was the implied question. I realised that the way I felt, must have been very similar to Barbara's experiences. I surrendered all control and entrusted the matter to the consultant. We agreed that I would have an operation in the near future.

The conclusion to this story does not belong here. Yet, I feel the story would be incomplete without it. After a considerable time, my fear and other emotions subsided, and my self-esteem re-established itself. At the same time, I hypothesised the cardiologist's vulnerability and his value patterns. Since, I have been able to start afresh with my investigations. The outcome of this search was startling. I visited three hospitals and had it confirmed that, as there was no deterioration in my heart valve, no operation was necessary. I was also told, to my considerable relief, that I could resume my normal life pattern.

When I met Barbara to discuss the publication of her case study, I showed her my epilogue to the story of 'Who do you think you are', displaying my identification with her emotions. We both had a good laugh.

During our sessions together I felt that I had Freddie's whole attention and this gave me confidence in him. Therefore, when he announced quite early on that 'change has already taken place', I believed him, although I was not sure what that change was. He referred often to the positive things I had achieved, not in spite of my background – which was my view – but because of it. This change in emphasis helped me to see that my lack of confidence has had not only a negative effect on my life, but also positive one, by providing the powerful motivation to prove myself.

Reading Freddie's account of my therapy, I realise that the two interventions that he describes as 'out of character' are the two that made the most impact on me. The first was 'Your problem is not your low self-esteem but your belief that you are the only person in the world to experience it and be ashamed of it'. On a rational level I know that everyone is vulnerable, yet when Freddie said this to me, it came as a revelation. I think that on an emotional level, I was convinced that no one else could feel as worthless and ashamed as I did. It seems unbelievable that I had not grasped the simple, obvious truth that people patronise, belittle, and dismiss others, because they themselves feel insecure. I had always tended to see everyone else as strong and myself as weak. Taking in the idea that others may feel as insecure as I do may helps to redress the balance. Feeling on more equal terms with my 'persecutors' perhaps I can begin to stand up for myself.

I have to admit that I was irritated to read Freddie's comment that he would have preferred me to arrive at the above conclusion without any prompting from him. If he had not acted 'out of character' to make this intervention I cannot imagine that I would have reached it on my own, however, obvious it may seem. I wonder how many other insights I have missed while Freddie (and my previous therapist) waited for me to reach conclusions without prompting.

The other intervention, which made an impact on me, followed my description of a lunch with two of my husband's friends. I had tried very hard to please them, for them to like me. I had felt really depressed, afterwards, about how desperate I still am for other peoples' approval. Freddie's suggestion that next time I should behave as if I did not want them to like me, not only made me laugh, but also made a deep impression on me. The startling idea that it might be possible to relate to others free from the anxiety of 'what do they think of me?' lodged itself deeply in my psyche. I hope it will bear fruit in due course.

Reading in print about how ashamed I am of my working-class origins, I realised that this is no longer true. I think that the need to hide the shame of having been humiliated by my father's sarcasm was so great that as an adult I transferred the shame to something more acceptable: my working-class background. I am now much less ashamed of this and of the way my father treated me.

When Freddie related the story of his heart surgery dilemma, I was quite shaken. His admission that the heart specialist had reduced his self-esteem to zero shook my confidence in him. Could I respect someone who could be made so small? Where was the mature, strong therapist I imagined him to be? On reflection, I admire his courage for telling me this story. I have come to believe that it was one of the most helpful things he did for me. If he can accept and reveal his vulnerability, perhaps I can do the same.

CONCLUSION

Barbara presented her problem as the fear of being 'found out'. This would cause her immense pain, and she was convinced that her entire personality would be annihilated. It would destroy her, if people would find out that she came from a working-class background, that her accent was acquired, and about her inadequate education.

Her value system was thus rigidified: in order to be somebody of value one must be middle-class and possess a university education. She also felt that her salvation rested in the discovery of her real self. Although Barbara had achieved a great deal in life, nothing satisfied her enough to accept her current self. In therapy, she was searching for what she called her 'real self', which was spontaneous and carefree. Yet, she also realised that this search could be an eternally futile one, since life is not limitless and she had to find meaning within those limitations. During the therapy, she became aware of her exaggerated and distorted negative perception of her self. Her contempt of her shame made her over-emotional and over-sensitive. Her fear and anxiety prevented her from seeing other people's vulnerabilities. All of these issues hindered her in creating intimate relationships.

4. Fear and Anxiety

Barbara could now challenge herself as to whether she always needed her rigid values and the approval of others. Perhaps she could find a meaning for herself in continuing her music studies and improving her personal relationships. I had faith in Barbara and gave her credit that her self-explorations would give her more insights. I hoped that she would come to accept herself, and would increasingly find more meaning to life. We both knew that some issues would remain and that others would re-emerge. We were also mindful that the residue of her sedimented issue of 'who do you think you are' would not disappear entirely. Yet, the awareness of it would make a difference.

5

Guilt

On the issue of experiencing guilt, I distinguish both in my personal life and in my professional relationship with clients between three types of guilt. Guilt relating to an action or thought which actually infringed our moral imperatives; imagined guilt, sometimes called neurotic guilt, which is guilt about some minor or illusory wrong-doing that is exaggerated and which we attribute to ourselves. Lastly, there is existential guilt which concerns our unfulfilled potential and which is an expression of our unavoidable anxiety of being. Whether this guilt remains in the background or whether it emerges into our awareness, I feel such guilt always accompanies us in our life and it is a futile exercise to try and eliminate it.

My experience of these three types is confirmed by existential thinkers and practitioners' views, such as May (1977), Spinelli (1989), van Deurzen-Smith (1988) and Yalom (1980). Every decision provokes anxiety, as there are infinite possibilities to choose from. Yalom writes, for example: 'Neurotic guilt emanates from imagined transgressions (or minor transgressions that are responded to in a disproportionately powerful manner ...) ... Real guilt flows from an actual transgression against another' (276-7). On the other hand, existential guilt, according to Yalom, is a 'transgression to oneself' which 'emanates from regret, from an awareness of unlived life, of the untapped possibilities within one' (320). Spinelli argues against the traditional psychoanalytical notion that guilt is caused by the psychic conflict between our unconscious and conscious drives. He argues that guilt 'is the threat to the individual's sense of being' (168). In other words, existential anxiety itself creates sometimes a neurotic anxiety about the threat and fear of the annihilation of our being.

When I think about choices in my own life, the most guilt-provoking situations that come to mind are part of my war experiences. While living in Nazi-occupied Budapest, I used false identity papers to prove my Aryan origins in order to escape deportation to a labour or concentration camp. I was lucky that I had access to these false papers

71

which no doubt saved several people's lives, including my own. I was also lucky in that I was able to distribute such papers to others, which could sometimes make a difference between life and death.

It was at the beginning of November 1944, on a very cold wintery day, when I met Hardy, a Jewish school colleague of mine. We both expressed surprise that we were free and able to meet in a street in Budapest. He took me to his parents, who by some accident had escaped being arrested. Despite bombings and police and Gestapo raids that were taking place, we managed to spend a joyful afternoon together. Just before the outbreak of the war, Hardy had returned to Budapest from a boarding school in England in order to be in a 'safer' place with his parents. We managed to joke about it and Hardy, who was a superb pianist, entertained us by playing popular jazz. It was a wonderful occasion, but also our last encounter. Before I left we agreed that in the next few days I would supply him and his parents with 'water-tight' sets of Aryan papers.

Early next morning I had to deliver false documents to some of my Yugoslav friends in the Swiss Embassy. I was twenty years old and I felt totally immune to the danger of the Hungarian Gestapo raids, certain that my documents would protect me. On top of that, I also felt confident that I had the capacity to perform these important tasks. I know now that I was not an 'important' person, but plainly an ignorant one for not realising that my chances of surviving a Gestapo investigation were practically nil. The day passed, and in the fervour of my 'important' tasks, like putting documents together and obtaining the necessary materials, I completely forgot about my promise to Hardy and his parents.

Two days later, when I remembered my promise, I assembled the papers in a panic and rushed to Hardy's home. I climbed up the stairs to their flat and suddenly a deadly silence struck me. There was no answer to the bell and then I heard some footsteps and the concierge appeared. Congierges were suspected of being Gestapo stooges, yet as soon as I saw him, I knew that he was a decent person. He had a solemn face and he said slowly 'Yes, they took them away last night'. I instantly escaped from the district, which I did very skilfully. In the evening, I began to think about what had really happened and suddenly I felt a shock-wave running through my body. I started to sweat and began trembling; I realised then that I could have saved the family by delivering the promised documents on time. A few months after this event, the occupation ended and joy overwhelmed me. For a long time, I completely banned this tragic incident from my mind. Indeed the whole incident merged with my unresolved grief about the Holocaust, which was pushed back in the midst of building up a new life, career and family.

Many years after these events when things were going well, the feeling of the shock wave started to reappear in my dreams. These nightmares appeared at irregular intervals and were as vivid and painful as the actual events. The feeling of the dream usually stayed with me all day long.

I analysed these dreams from all angles. The most comfortable analyses pointed to a neurotic element in my guilt. After all, the Gestapo raid took place the day I promised to deliver the documents and if I had delivered them to my friends on time, I could have been arrested with them. I also analysed what my responsibility was in this sorrowful episode. Was it my responsibility to rescue everybody? But there was a darker side to these explorations: were my feeling of self-importance, my self-esteem, more important than Hardy's family? Was I driven to prove that I was somebody, forgetting my friends in the midst of this frenzied activity? Was this real wrongdoing? I could not reconcile my actions, or placate myself and accept that I had no answer. While those dreams gradually disappeared, the problem of my own guilt was only solved by acceptance of the fact that I could never find an answer to this question.

As far as existential guilt is concerned, I have come to the conclusion that there are never situations or decisions which cannot be challenged. This is the guilt that is always lurking in the back of our minds about unfulfilled potential.

CASE STUDY

Thirty six year old Kane moved to England from South Africa at the age of eleven. At the time of the therapy, he lived in London with his South African partner. His father left his mother when Kane was a young boy and his mother remarried. Kane had great respect for his stepfather, who expected 'perfection' from him in every way.

Kane was a computer analyst, but his real love was music. He found his computer work repetitive and uninteresting. His desire was to become a well-known musician and to leave computers altogether. He was very much devoted to Suka, his partner. He had an especially trustworthy loving attachment to his late mother-in-law. The therapy was about his guilt in not reciprocating the love shown to him by others, his fear of rejection, the sexual abuse he had suffered as a boy and his feelings of abandonment by those close to him. He would revisit these feelings repeatedly when he felt frustrated in not fulfilling his feelings of devotion.

THERAPY

First Session and Framework

Kane presented himself well and gave the impression of a young, energetic and intelligent person. As is usual, the first session was about acquainting myself with his presenting problem, but more importantly to find out whether we suited each other in the therapeutic realm.

In the first thirty minutes, he was able to unburden himself of problems, large and small, either about his work or about his girlfriend Suka. He felt angry with himself that he could not solve some of the problems with the computer system at work. This provoked anger and contempt towards himself. The underlying feeling, however, was of his inferiority because only as a creative person could he perceive himself as a worthwhile individual.

I felt the need to acquire insight into his world-view. The anger that Kane expressed served as an opportunity to focus on his present emotions and I felt this could reveal some of his values and behaviour patterns. I thought this would not only enable me to relate to him empathetically but also to prompt Kane to challenge his ambiguities. All these would be essential for both of us in deciding whether to enter into a serious therapeutic relationship. He gave me the impression of a lively yet self-reflecting person. I felt therefore that my empathic and challenging stance was correct for Kane and would give him a glimpse of how the therapy could develop. As his issue now was his anger and boredom towards his work, I prompted him to explore this anger.

Kane felt frustrated about not being able to fulfil his overwhelming desire to be creative in music. He showed anger at the boredom he had to endure in such trivial work as computer analysis, only for the sake of material gain. He felt it was a complete waste of his time and energies.

I contemplated our possible therapeutic relationship. I was not only interested in but also empathic towards Kane. I also felt that through his capacity to listen and to be logically self-reflecting, he would soon be able to analyse his own world-view. As a result, I proposed that if he chose to work with me, he should ask me all manners of questions, before settling our contract. I for my part explained that I would be pleased to work with him. In response to his questions, I pointed out that our future sessions would be very similar to this introductory session. I would carry on prompting him to acquaint himself with some of those issues that he might not be aware of and to reacquaint him with other already known issues in order to look at them anew and experience them again. In the process of this, he asked me some personal questions. I am always prepared to disclose all at the introductory session. I strongly believe that a client has the absolute right to know those things about me which are relevant to our therapy before committing himself to total disclosure of his inner feelings.

We agreed to the usual contractual arrangement, at Kane's suggestion, of six sessions and two review sessions, despite my inclination towards a minimum of twelve sessions. This difference was due to Kane's financial situation. We agreed to total commitment on both sides. This entailed the likelihood of pain and joy, whatever the therapeutic discussion and disclosure would provoke. We also agreed to confidentiality on my part. Kane on the other hand, was at liberty to be open and talk to anyone, should he feel the need to do so. Time keeping and commitment to the process of therapy for both parties was essential to our agreement. After he left, I took some notes that his guilt about his inability to accomplish his aspiration in respect of his career might be an existential guilt at not fulfilling totally his potential concerning his music talent. I thought that he might be able to challenge himself and explore whether he could always strive for total achievement.

THERAPEUTIC ENCOUNTER
Perfection

In subsequent sessions, Kane began to unfold his story. His father was an architect but unfortunately an alcoholic. It, therefore, fell upon his mother to provide for the family's everyday needs. In due course, his father left them and his mother remarried. He was eleven years old when he arrived in London with his mother and stepfather. I tried to prompt him to narrate his experiences and to express his emotions in respect of his arrival in a strange country with his new stepfather. He loved but also feared his stepfather. 'He is a very clever and diligent man. He likes me, but he expects a lot from me'. I was waiting for further developments in his story. After a silence he continued 'As much as I tried to please him, nothing was good enough for him. When I proudly brought home good examination results, he scolded me for not doing better still'.

'So you had to be perfect?' I prompted him.

He enlarged on this and spoke of his fear of asking his stepfather any favours, which would reveal his own inadequacy. For example, his stepfather was an expert handyman and on one occasion, Kane had asked him to repair a domestic appliance. His stepfather repaired the appliance perfectly, in a very short time. Just as his stepfather was leaving the room, he scolded Kane for his inability to do the same job. This was confirmation for Kane of his 'shameful inadequacies'.

As I challenged him, Kane recognised how deeply this deprecating pattern influenced him in all of his own experiences and achievements. I felt that Kane was greatly surprised at his discovery and I prompted him to explore further his overwhelming desire to be perfect in everything.

'Do you mean that I am belittling myself, because everything that I am doing is not perfect enough for me?' Kane said. I paused, I was afraid that I might have put words in his mouth, prematurely. This, however, proved not to be the case. Kane latched onto the word 'perfect' and exhaustively explored his attachment to this value.

In the next session, I urged him to challenge himself about his generally disparaging view of himself. If he was right, how could he have achieved good enough 'O' and 'A' levels to go to university and leave with a good degree? He also challenged his own behaviour in withdrawing from any task that threatened his need to be perfect. At this stage of the therapy, Kane had become aware of his aspiration in life to be perfect in all aspects of his actions, otherwise his self-esteem would drop, and deep feelings of guilt would ensue.

The Abuse

In one of the following sessions, Kane recalled his feelings of pain concerning an incident of abuse. When he was nine years old, a boy who was several years older enticed him to go to his house where he sexually abused him.

As he narrated the story, I did not perceive the pain. It somehow did not reverberate or touch me. I ventured to say: 'I think this must have been a hideously painful experience, yet I do not detect the pain'.

Kane paused for few moments, swallowed hard, then continued: 'That is not the pain I feel now. What hurts me is my father. I never felt any love from him, he neglected us, and he used to come home drunk and beat my mother. After what happened, I ran home for help and solace. I found my father and hoped that by unburdening myself I would find comfort and relief. Instead, he ruthlessly beat me. That is what really hurts'.

In this session, Kane experienced the pain and loneliness of a helpless, thoroughly abandoned child. I considered the situation carefully and I was afraid that I would intervene prematurely. Somehow, I felt there was something missing for me. I contemplated what had happened with the pain emanating from the abuse itself. Yet, I did not want to bring up this subject as this was not Kane's agenda at the moment. I also hesitated because of the time limitation of our therapy. I thought that if Kane was ready to bring up this subject he would do so himself, or he would ask for another module. As it happened there was no other module and, indeed, Kane never brought up in detail his experience of the actual abuse.

I asked him gently: 'Kane, am I correct in assuming that you never experienced any fatherly tenderness?' 'Never', he replied. 'What about from your mother? Were you ever hugged and caressed?' I asked. 'I probably received affection in my early youth, but my mother was totally submissive to my natural father and she is the same with my stepfather'.

I clearly remember my concern in this session about the time limitation of the therapy. Although it was only the second session, I was unsure of the wisdom of our short contract – six sessions, plus two review sessions. I contemplated whether Kane would have to renegotiate another module of twelve sessions before the ending of this module, and that maybe even that would have to be renegotiated. Yet, I knew also that in therapy there are very few predictable things and many surprises. As will be seen from what follows, my predictions were contradicted by events.

Before the end of the session, I asked Kane whether there was any loving experience that came to his mind. Without hesitation, he answered, 'Suka, my partner, and her mother'.

Guilt and Love

The following week Kane brought up the issue of his deep feelings of guilt about his treatment of his late mother-in-law. He had met his partner, Suka, at the age of eighteen at university. They had fallen passionately in love and moved to Kane's home, where his mother and stepfather had reluctantly accepted Suka. She came from the same ethnic and religious background as Kane, but was considered by his family as unacceptably 'lower class'. The attitude of Kane's parents eventually resulted in a complete breakdown of their relationship. Suka had to leave the house, but not before highly charged anger and panic-stricken emotions errupted. Suka vented her feelings using household articles as missiles to break most of the windows in the house.

For a year after Suka moved out, Kane remained with his parents, but they could no longer communicate with each other. The one thing Kane and Suka both shared was a feeling of loneliness and emptiness, which eventually overcame all else. Kane carried on with his studies and moved in with Suka, who shared a house with her mother who had had to work hard to make ends meet. She was, however, a person of great compassion and empathy who would do all she could to make her daughter happy. She also treated Kane as a part of her family. She not only showed love and care for Kane, but she also helped him for years to finance his university studies. This was no small achievement in view of her meagre financial circumstances.

Kane felt not only enormous gratitude, but also a deep-seated love and respect towards his mother-in-law. He tried to reciprocate this with as much love and care as was in his power. When his mother-in-law fell ill, both he and Suka cared for her and nursed her day and night. After all, Kane found in both of them what he had really missed in his life: love and affection.

Kane now felt ready to discuss and reveal his feeling of extreme guilt. 'We found a flat and moved out of Suka's home. Her mother became ill and wanted to come and live with us. Despite my agreement, after an agonising discussion with Suka, we felt that this was impractical for the time being. We both visited her very frequently, but she became weaker and weaker. Unknown to us at the time, she was terminally ill.

One day I went on one of my regular visits to Suka's mother. I rang the doorbell; and I banged hard on the door, but there was no response. A panicky, sickly feeling came over me. I alerted some of her neighbours, and together we forced our way in to her home. There was a horrifying scene; Suka's mother had put an end to her life in an indescribably extreme manner. 'I still cannot get over it' he said.

'Often I cannot fall asleep without this abominable image before my eyes. I still feel greatly distressed at my heartless behaviour. We should have taken her to our flat – now it is too late'.

A long silence followed. I empathised with Kane's pain in the silence and wondered if it were possible ever for me to really feel his hurt in the way, he felt it. Then I intervened, asking Kane whether it was possible for him to elaborate on what he meant by being 'heartless'? He replied that he felt overwhelmingly guilty and ashamed that he had not reciprocated the love and kindness shown to him by Suka's mother when he had the opportunity to do so. He considered himself undeserving of any compassion and felt abandoned, lost, helpless, and unable to trust anyone. His self-esteem was at an all time low.

I then encouraged Kane to explore the relationship between his self-esteem and his desire to reciprocate love and perfection, of which he had become strongly aware in the previous session. It did not take Kane long to challenge himself and to draw the connection between these aspects of himself. In other words, he realised that his inadequacy and guilt were dependent on his overpowering need to express with total devotion and loyalty his affection towards his late mother-in-law. To be good enough did not suffice.

In one of the sessions that followed, Kane was exploring his emotions of love and guilt, not only towards his late mother-in-law, but also towards Suka. He spoke about his dependence on Suka and how he trusted and profoundly loved her. Despite this, he felt guilty for often not being with her when she needed him most. At this stage, I sensed that Kane was overcome by many different emotions – love, guilt, fear, deprecation, and anger – all directed against himself. Nevertheless, guilt mixed with love was what he spoke about; guilt relentlessly pursued him. While I believed that Kane felt quite emotional – guilty, abandoned and helpless – I wondered whether his guilt was an existential issue about his unfulfilled potential or legitimate guilt. How much did his compulsive drive for perfection contribute to his predicament?

I did not want to side-track the emotional moment and I ventured to ask: 'Kane, could you think of any other situation, place or circumstance where you experience this feeling of abandonment that you feel now?' 'Abandonment?', he queried. Then after a long pensive silence, he asked: 'Do you want me to go back to my childhood?'

I carefully considered whether Kane perceived my intervention as an intention to take him back to the past to reveal something unbeknown to him. Yet, that was the last thing I wanted him to do. I did not want Kane to think that by finding cause or linkage, he could solve his problems. My quest was very much aimed at finding an example that would more clearly illuminate Kane's feelings in the present. I also knew that in order to explore Kane's behaviour patterns I needed to tune out for the moment from this tense and emotional dialogue. Therefore, I responded 'No, I would like you to concentrate on the present and your current perception of your issues'. I pictured in my mind the scene when young Kane ran to his father in order to be rescued, instead of which his father abandoned him. I probed him and asked him to explore those feeling of abandonment by his father. Kane then continued to explore aloud his feelings of distrust and helplessness.

'Many times in my life, I lost trust in others and in myself, too', he said. 'What do you feel is happening between us in relation to this topic? I asked. 'I feel there is trust between us, so I can say anything I want' he said. 'Trust'? I queried again. 'Yes trust' was his emphatic reply.

It appeared to me that this trust, along with love and care, was the building block that Kane needed for his self-esteem. It seemed to me that Kane had vested all his love and care, which he had not experienced from his family, in Suka and her mother. Moreover, this love and affection had to be all encompassing and 'perfect'. As it was impossible for him to fulfil this entirely, he often experienced guilt and shame.

Creativity, Love of Music

Kane had just returned from the U.S., where he had been partly on holiday. The main purpose of his visit, however, was to see if he could embark on a career of writing lyrics and performing as a musician. He came back disappointed. Now, he really could not see how he would be able to leave his career as a computer analyst. Since the beginning of the therapy, we were both aware of Kane's issue with his career. He believed in his talent and he was convinced that he could only fulfil his potential through his creative work.

In this session, Kane expressed his frustration and anger about his failure to establish a foothold in the music field in the U.S. After a while, I urged him to analyse his issues in greater detail. I asked him who he was angry with, what his sadness was about; and what was the dream lost in America? I immediately reprimanded myself for making such a long and complex intervention, encompassing so many issues and emotions. Usually, I have a well-thought-out habit of focusing on one emotion at a time, as I find that all emotions are in any case connected with each other. I thought it would have been easier for Kane to concentrate on one emotion and thus reveal his world-view to himself.

As it happened, Kane broke through my internal polemic by saying, 'I am angry with myself and sad about myself. I want to be able to work creatively and to be accepted for it. I am thoroughly bored in my computer work. There is no creativity there'. Soon Kane began to connect this to his self-esteem and to the loneliness he tried so hard to avoid. He investigated at length the importance of creativity for himself. 'Kane, would it not be possible for you, having shown so much ability and ingenuity in your life, to explore whether you could put your creative mind to use in your work with computers?' I suggested. Kane looked at me in great amazement: evidently, this had not occurred to him before.

The following week, however, the idea had taken root. He spoke of his achievements in his work place. He planned to change his job and to become a freelance analyst where he could use his creativity to write special software. I felt that Kane wanted to tell me something. With a half-smiling and half-worried look on his face he told me eventually that something in our relationship bothered him. I remained silent. I felt that we knew each other reasonably well, so I was surprised that he had challenged our trusting relationship. In a way, he did just that.

'In our culture, one's name is a very important part of a trusting relationship' he said. 'In other words, it is of considerable importance for me to know that when I truly trust somebody, he should know my first name properly. We are now almost at the end of the therapy and you still mispronounce my name'.

This surprised me greatly. Yet, I knew he was right. I also knew that in general I had a great problem with pronouncing unfamiliar names, which is an unresolved problem of mine. I suffer a lot from this, especially in classes, where my students rightly expect me to memorise their names. Unfortunately, although I know that this can harm my relationship with my students, I usually forget to ask the simple question 'What is your name, I am sorry I have forgotten it'. Yet now, without hesitation, I said: 'I am extremely sorry Kane, that is my general problem. In addition, I must thank you very much for being able honestly to tell me what you feel. I appreciate it and I feel that is your contribution to me'. I felt that after this session, our mutual trust had been further cemented.

In the penultimate session, we discussed our feelings about the therapy. I expected that Kane would want to negotiate at least another module. There were issues that we had hardly touched upon and I had the feeling that Kane would welcome a further opportunity to discuss this. I was mistaken. Kane was clear about his intention. He referred to our many discussions and to our first session and said 'I was working hard during the sessions and between the sessions and I hope I will be able to continue this work after the therapy'. We discussed his relentlessly emerging guilt and low self-esteem and we both realised that these issues might re-emerge from time to time and that a residue might always remain with him.

We agreed that in the final session, we would give feedback to each other; what we expected from this therapy and what we would both 'take with us' from our association with one another. Kane began 'For years, I have been in therapy. I have indeed gained some insight, but I have also experienced irritation, particularly about therapists' passivity. Now my feeling is that I learned a great deal in these six sessions'. 'Could you enlarge on this?' I asked. 'It was a real revelation for me that my behaviour pattern is to such an extent dependent on my own attitudes' he said. 'I further realise that my belief that I have to be "perfect" in every situation is often the cause of my self-deprecating attitude. I recognise that in general I reciprocated my mother-in-law's kindness as much as I was able to. I cared for her kindly and thoughtfully. In fact, I believe I did all that was in my power. I also became aware of the fact that I could not only be creative in music, but could also regard my work as a computer programme analyst as creative'. Kane decided to change the way he worked. He would now become a freelance consultant, but still in computers. 'In this capacity', Kevin concluded, 'I can still be creative and innovative'.

'What will you do with your occasional guilt about not reciprocating love, as well as your low self-esteem?' I asked him. Kane was in good spirits and said: 'I will deal with them myself, and I can always call you if I experience great difficulties'. In my mind, I gave credit to Kane that he was capable of doing all this. Yet I was not convinced everything would go as smoothly as he had outlined. After a pause, I said 'It is gratifying for me to hear that you have experienced some insight changes during our relationship. However, it is of equal importance for me to hear that you acknowledge that some issues will remain and that you are determined to work by yourself on them. The fact that you know I am here for you, should you need some support after a while, reassures me'.

I told Kane that even in this brief period I felt grateful that we could converse empathetically and trustingly and that I was impressed how we had both kept to our deep commitment and thus developed a mutual respect. This in itself helped Kane to plunge straight into revealing both his world-view and his rigid beliefs. Kane had worked very hard indeed between his therapy sessions and had almost literally dived in to explore his world-view.

6

Sadness

This chapter will illustrate my own and Sophie's experiences of sadness, and her therapy. At the beginning of this section, I will relate my own encounters, followed by some reflections about sadness in general. Sophie has written her own account of the therapy, which is preceded by a case account written by me. Finally, there will be a summary pointing out the differences between the two perceptions.

MY OWN EXPERIENCE

Suffering and trouble belong to life as much as faith and death. None of these can be subtracted from life without destroying its meaning. To subtract trouble, death, fate, and suffering from life would mean stripping life of its form and shape. Only under the hammer blows of fate, in the white heat of suffering does life gain shape and form ... Human life can be fulfilled not only in creating and enjoying, but also in suffering. (Frankl:1955:106, 111)

Apart from my experience of sadness stemming from the losses in my life, losing my home, a large part of my family etc., I also experience sadness in the knowledge that all my relationships with others are of a transient nature. While I can comfort myself that this type of sadness is something that is part of human existence and one of the givens of the world, I can still not discard and ignore it. I also feel sometimes that sadness has a function in my life: a feeling to be emptied and to provide conditions for refilling the emptiness with new energy, and allow me to reappraise my life. Sometimes I also look forward to this state of emptiness, even compared to happiness.

However, when I wake up from a nightmare about my deepest losses, sadness totally overwhelms me. Then I try remembering the above quote by Frankl and try to find solace in those words. I know

I have hit the 'bottom' of my loneliness, when I have lost most of my precious meanings. Mostly, however, just by focusing on obvious areas of meaning, for example, family, work etc, and on creation of new meanings and projects in life, I feel that somehow I will emerge from this dismal place.

Yet, certain overwhelming memories of my experiences sometimes evoke such deep-seated feelings of sorrow that the experience makes me feel there is insufficient time left in my life to grieve and to lament those losses. I refer mainly to those, which stem from my wartime experiences – the shock of the Holocaust and related events. Again, many times, I am astounded by how much energy life can still provide me with in order to maintain optimism in my relationship to my family and others and serve me with meaning in the world.

REFLECTIONS ON SADNESS

Sadness is distinct from other emotions due to the nature of its duration. It is less intense than any other emotion and usually lasts a longer period of time. It can also be considered as an all-pervading mood, generally comprising being down-hearted, lonely, and feeling isolated. It is predominantly connected with loss, though not necessarily connected with grief for another individual. It may relate to the loss of love, of joy, of enthusiasm, of loyalty, of contentment, of pride, etc. In other words, the loss of meaning of a certain purpose in life usually goes hand in hand with the loss of one's self-esteem.

When sadness arrives at an extreme point in one's life, when life becomes meaningless and there is no hope of regaining one's self-esteem, then depression may ensue. Meaninglessness is a void that goes beyond sadness when an individual loses all hope. Meaning and meaninglessness are discussed in more detail, within the context of the existential givens, in Chapter One. Yet, it is important to note how meaning intrinsically interconnects with all emotions, in this case with sadness. Sadness is about something that is connected with loss of a meaning we much value. This in turn may disclose one's self-esteem and one's attitude towards differing choices. That is how through meaning or meaninglessness we reveal part of our world-view.

To reiterate a question asked in the first chapter, we could question what the purpose is of disclosure of one's world-view. It is the awareness of this world-view, which makes individuals realise and challenge discrepancies and ambiguities in their behaviour pattern. Sophie's account, follow, will demonstrate this in great detail. It will be seen from that even meaning has its price. Her identity was defined by her fixed sedimentation in strictly believing in certain values and behaviour. When she became frustrated as a result of being unable to conform to these 'imperatives', she paradoxically fell into a state of meaninglessness.

Yet it is important to note how this meaning and meaninglessness interact with an individual client's emotions, self-esteem, choice and insecurities, and also the possibility of making decisions and choosing – albeit only within the givens of the world. In Sophie's case, one of her important aims in life was to maintain her virginity until her marriage and to stick to her family's strict moral standards. The slightest threat to this strict moral attitude threw her into despair: she would collapse and her self-esteem would shatter. Sophie felt lonely; her life was meaningless. Yet when she became aware of her world-view, she was able to work it through and challenge her rigid belief system. Then, and only then, was she able to think of slowly modifying her conception of boundaries. She realised that a boundary is important, but that life has its own vicissitudes. She recognised that she could change her attitude to life and modify or substitute this meaning. The same applied to Sophie's rigid convictions about sexual matters.

Sadness is more often than not considered a negative emotion, yet it has many positive elements. It could be argued that without sadness there would be no joy or happiness. Can we imagine living without mourning the death of a loved one, or responding with empathy to the sorrow of another? As has been seen from my own experiences, sadness can in a paradoxical way not only cause suffering but also accommodate happiness.

SOPHIE'S CASE HISTORY

From the moment I began researching aspects of emotions, Sophie's case instantly came to mind. Whenever I thought of emotions I could not forget the lasting impression Sophie's deep-seated sadness and, paradoxically, her optimistic nature. It is many years since I last saw Sophie in therapy. I contacted her a few months ago to ask if she would be interested to contribute to this Chapter and I found her willing and happy to cooperate. She reminded me of her therapy notes that she kept in the form of a book, which would now be a great help. At that time I still practised open-ended therapy, as opposed to the time-limited modular approach. The difference of the two models is described in detail in the previous chapters.

Sophie and I worked together for over four years, when she decided to move and return to her studies for an MBA, and we agreed that I would refer her to another therapist. She felt that her cooperation in this chapter would be a valuable experience that would help in her further development. We have met several times and agreed that we each write our own version of the therapy and compare notes to highlight any differences in our perceptions.

Sex

When Sophie first appeared on my doorstep she appeared shy but determined, as though she knew exactly what she wanted. She looked small in build, slightly overweight, but agile and feminine. She walked towards my consulting room as if she knew the way. At that time, it was on the lower ground-floor. My first impression was that, despite her shyness, she was well able to tell her story. Furthermore, she had no problem at all in correcting me when my intervention did not fit in with her perception.

She began to recount her experiences at her part-time Degree Course in business studies. Sophie was thirty years old and worked as a successful personnel director. I pondered what had driven her to continue her education and what was the reason that she had not proceeded with her higher education at an earlier age. Therefore, as I prompted her to expand on this subject, surprisingly, she almost reprimanded me that she wanted to stay with the core subject. She simply wanted to keep to her agenda and not delve into her early past. She said that she did not want to be 'side-tracked'. This was an expression often used by her. I was taken aback by her remark, but I also felt good about it, as this was a sign of trust in me. I also feared that I might have 'pushed' her prematurely. This, if true, would have been my issue.

She then spoke about Ian. He was twenty four years older then her. He lived in the country and was married with two children. She was in a relationship with him, but recently she suspected that he was unsure of his feelings towards her. She was certain that even if he was not deceitful, something strange was going on in their relationship. Sophie loved him dearly and was suffering from the added pain of feeling let-down. Also the whole affair was well outside her boundaries. This made her feel guilty and immensely sad. In many of the following sessions we explored Sophie's emotions towards Ian, her previous relationships, her attitude to sex, parents and family.

Sophie was bought up in a family where sex, masturbation and talk of intercourse were taboo. There were no explicit prohibitions and Sophie could not recollect any reprimands or threats that would indicate such a conservative attitude. Yet, the traditional ethos and morality of this devout Calvinist family left a lasting impression on her. Sophie had not experienced penetrative sex as this was against her beliefs. She was, however, able to embark on petting and kissing with several previous boyfriends.

With Ian, she even went so far as to allow him to have everything but penetrative sex. She could not even contemplate the thought of penetration, although she enjoyed everything else. Immense feelings of guilt and total dread of penetration accompanied all these acts. The fear of an erect penis that could penetrate was constantly inhibiting her. This stopped any meaningful or full sexual relationship with a man. Masturbation was prohibited and she often felt frustrated. The fear of losing Ian, of loneliness and total insecurity characterised the part of the therapy.

In the therapy, Sophie focused on sexual issues but she also connected this to her other issues. It became evident that her sexual issues were connected with her interpersonal relationships and perhaps had a bearing on the issue of her epileptic seizures.

The whole question of sexuality was wrapped in a certain mystery. I felt that there was a similarity in her approach in articulating her story in therapy with her relationship with her ex-boyfriends. She really wanted to 'open-up' and tell me all about her sexuality. Yet in a way she felt that she could not. At times, when she felt 'side-tracked', even by herself, on another subject, she reminded herself and in a disciplined manner promptly returned to sexuality.

My interventions were very cautious. I prompted her to carry on telling her story and encouraged her to challenge herself. I facilitated her examination of her desire to have a meaningful relationship, although at the same time she shied away from it. She was thirty years old and in spite of her wide-ranging general knowledge and high intelligence, she still knew very little about sexuality.

I did not want to take risks with Sophie at this juncture of the therapy. I tried to avoid premature challenges and I encouraged the flow of the narrative. I knew she recognised my empathy towards her feelings and my understanding of her behaviour. I hoped that this was sufficient encouragement for Sophie to challenge and observe her discrepancies and her contradictions. Sophie had struggled to divulge her sexuality, amidst an air of deep-seated sorrow and sadness. Behind all this woe, there was strength, optimism, and a strong desire for her to find a way in life.

I often had to struggle with my own feelings. I not only felt empathy towards Sophie, but sometimes I almost felt responsible for her, as if she was my own daughter. I thought that having three daughters of my own made this more of an issue for me. I knew, however, that I had to suspend this feeling so that I remained alert to her from a wider perspective. I knew that when I tuned into her pain I also had to free myself from her issues so that I could see her ambiguities, which helped my occasional interventions.

Slowly Sophie gained confidence and trust in our relationship, and for the first time she told me of an incident with sexual connotations. She was five years old when one night she woke up. She walked through the dark corridor, to the bathroom. On the way, she found the door of her parents' bedroom slightly ajar and sought help from her mother. As she entered her parents' bedroom, she saw that her 'big' father (in reality he was only 5"1') was 'climbing' on to her mother. She saw his penis just as it penetrated her mother. Sophie froze and stood still as a statue. She could not comprehend what she saw. She turned and ran to her room. There she jumped into bed and hid under her blankets. Her mother, with a face red with embarrassment, came into her room, turned the light on, and asked what Sophie had wanted. When she got no answer, she disappeared without saying a word, without an explanation or a word of guidance.

As she expanded on the story, Sophie still felt very angry with her mother. She would have expected warmth, compassion, guidance and sympathy. She was convinced that her parents were unable to listen to her and could not or had not wanted to perceive her pain and insecurity. She needed explanations, consolation and loving, tactile contact from her parents. Instead, she felt totally excluded, rejected, and isolated.

In general, in Sophie's perception she was excluded from her parents' emotional life. In her later cognition, she blamed this situation as the cause for her fear of some aspects of her sexuality. She also believed that she was treated 'differently' from her younger brother.

I made a mental note of this. The fact that she blamed so much on her perception of the past could serve as a good metaphor for further explorations of her world-view. As it transpired, her loneliness, isolation and fear of rejection, were also intrinsically interconnected with a dread of epileptic seizures, interpersonal relationships, and problems with her boundaries.

In subsequent sessions, she spoke about her struggle with her own sexual arousal as well as her value system. She was immensely passionate, but believed that sexual passion was sinful. After all, this was against her family ethos. She thought of masturbation as prohibited terrain and she had very limited physiological knowledge of it or indeed of sexuality in general. She had had sexual experiences with her boyfriends. She usually guided their hands to her genitals and felt good about it, yet guilt and sadness ensued. On one occasion, she struggled not to be penetrated but her passion was so great that she almost lost the battle. Her boyfriend was about to penetrate her. Fortunately for her, she heard the noise of the key turning in the lock, as her parents unexpectedly arrived home. Sophie and her boyfriend had to get dressed quickly, and fled.

The beginning of the therapy was characterised by the great sorrow of abandonment. Ian declared that his wife had discovered Sophie's existence. They had to end their relationship. Sophie doubted Ian's story and felt ambiguous about his motivation. Yet, despite her frequent bouts of depression and numerous calls to the Samaritans, and to me, she was still able to challenge herself.

Could she somehow shake her rigid belief of what was right and what was wrong for a well-behaved girl? She realised that for her sex and masturbation were prohibited – in her own words: 'good girls don't do this sort of thing'. Could she successfully challenge her overriding preoccupation with Ian? Could she find different values to masturbation and sexuality? Could she add a new meaning to her life?

In subsequent sessions, Sophie managed to see the connection between her values and her self-esteem. When she transgressed her value system, she felt lost, guilty, depressed and sad. At such times, she had been disapproved of by herself and others. Her self-esteem sank to zero. In order to move from this depressed state, she needed some achievable meaning in her life through which she, and others, could accept her and which had led to positive approval in the past. She also felt that our relationship had some meaning, as she experienced empathy that she had rarely found before our therapy sessions.

Epileptic Seizures

When things went very wrong Sophie used to fall into a depressed state; she felt her life was totally meaningless. In desperation, she used to telephone the Samaritans.

We explored these feelings of desperation, sorrow, and sadness, which were very closely connected with her lack of self-esteem. She was eight years old when her parents and grandmother drove her to church. They were quarrelling amongst themselves, and somehow Sophie felt that she was responsible for reconciling them. It was Easter Sunday and it was especially troubling for Sophie that on this day of all days she could not intervene and keep the peace. 'I was always responsible for keeping the peace between my parents and grandmother. I had always, as far as I can remember, had to reassure my parents and look after them. In the context of the strictly Calvinist family ethos where the father's function is to be the authority, my role as a child was paradoxical'.

When her parents and grandmother argued, she felt she had to be her mother's peacemaker. Sophie perceived that she was expected to be a perfectionist, especially by her father. Her mother would rarely contradict her father. Therefore, when Sophie thought that she was not 'perfect', she felt useless.

The following morning, she went to the kitchen, leaned over a chair and had her first epileptic seizure. 'One moment I was standing by the cooker, next I was lying on the cold linoleum. Every time I lifted my head, it was filled with dizziness'. Her parents called a doctor. He left a prescription and Sophie went to bed, to sleep. The rest of the family went to church.

She could never forget the feeling of neglect and the sorrow of it. 'How could they do this, how could they leave me alone?' There was no physical pain but the emotional torment was intolerable. There was no one with whom to discuss what had happened to her. Her sentiments were similar but more intense than that feeling of neglect and traumatic reaction she experienced when she witnessed her parents' having sex at the age of five. She spoke of her parents who were supposed to protect and love her, but who instead obliterated all those issues that were problematic for them.

From the time of her seizure Sophie's life changed completely. She became increasingly withdrawn. She had no desire to mix socially. She was afraid 'they' would find out that she, this hopeless, useless little girl, could expect nothing better each day than to have a seizure.

6. Sadness

During this period, I again struggled hard with my feelings. This was not a case of a temporary depressive state with the accompanying loss of meaning that would soon be recaptured. This was a constant fear and trepidation, and I could not avoid identifying with her. I again felt as if it could have happened within my own family. Yet, I also felt that just by speaking about it, Sophie was able to be totally free and honest in her revelations and thus something happened to both of us. A true mutual bond of trust developed between us.

We discussed the physiological and psychological effects of epilepsy. Sophie concluded that in her case the seizure could have been triggered off by both biological and emotional factors. Nevertheless, it was a real and disagreeable physical illness.

Boundaries

It will be recalled that we agreed our boundaries at the onset of the therapy. We agreed the time and 'space', as well as confidentiality and commitment, from both parties.

Due to an unforeseen change to the structure of the house where I practise, a breach of the therapeutic boundary had occurred. Some rebuilding work was being undertaken at the house. It was necessary because of this to move my consulting room from the lower ground floor to the ground floor. She regarded this as a change of 'space' in breach of our original contract which outlined the position of the consulting room. She, therefore, felt deeply that our contract had been violated. Sophie believed that I did not esteem her and that I did not empathise with her feelings. I was surprised as I had taken it for granted that Sophie would understand my situation and that we would come to some arrangement which accommodated the changed circumstances. I just could not grasp the depth of her emotion; that this change provoked such anger and devastation in Sophie. She expressed her feelings clearly. She reminded me of our commitments and insisted that I was obliged to keep to our agreement.

Concurrent with these events, she discussed her fears of the recurrence of her epileptic seizures. Her anxiety about that and the notion of abandonment made my own feelings towards her even more empathic. I felt that I was probably overstepping the boundaries in my feelings towards her. I fought to keep my sympathy in check, as I drifted into over-identifying with her pain. I had experienced a multitude of somewhat contradictory feelings. I was pleased that she was able to vent her feelings so spontaneously and vehemently. Uncomfortable as it was for me, in the strictest context of the framework, she was right. We discussed this issue, session after session. I revealed all my feelings and thoughts about the problem. I apologised, but it was still 'touch and go' that Sophie would remain in therapy with me.

Only after Sophie succeeded in exploring the general issue of boundaries in relation to her world-view was our trusting relationship restored. Sophie perceived my failure to keep strictly to our contract as a rejection. She felt that I did not listen to her, had abandoned her, was inconsiderate of her emotions, and acted in exactly the same way as her family and indeed the rest of the world acted towards her. In other words, I belittled her.

It was a painful period for both of us. It challenged her core values. She gradually realised that her values relating to interpersonal relationships were grounded in the idea of total perfectionism and dogmatic absolutism. She expected from her family total devotion, total understanding, and total consideration. Good enough parenting was not acceptable. In her view, much the same applied to our therapy.

It had again taken great many sessions for Sophie to be able to express her sorrow and real sadness for not having received the love, which she expected. She felt that the absence of 'the ideal relationship' and the threat of rejection could have been contributory factors in her seizures. The result of the seizures created a void in her towards any emotions she could feel. Her attacks were akin to a release from all her emotions. Surprisingly, while I considered the possibility of an epileptic seizure during a therapeutic session I had no fear of it occurring. She often spoke of her meaningless depression and her desperate attempt to escape from 'all this'. Many a time, she had long conversations with the Samaritans. Despite all this, our sessions were always vibrant and interesting, often humorous, as she is blessed with a great sense of humour. Moreover, gratifyingly for both of us, she was at times able to emerge from her feeling of meaninglessness and find some purpose in her life. We discussed different meanings in our lives such as work, interpersonal relationships, and even the possibility of different a direction in her studies.

Slowly, gradually, but with great persistence and at times with real pain, Sophie challenged her perfectionist values. She began to question whether she could expect from other people, or indeed her own family, that devotion which she believed she deserved. She came to understand that, like every one else, I had made mistakes, as I was also human.

SOPHIE'S STORY: BY SOPHIE

When I first read Freddie's draft of this Chapter, and found some discrepancies between our interpretations, I wanted to correct his mistakes in a similar fashion to the way I corrected him when we were working together. Frequently he would say 'correct me if I'm wrong, but I have a hunch that ...' and almost as frequently my response commenced with something like 'well, yes and no' or 'not quite', before I proceeded to explain which section of his statement was correct and which was not.

I have one further comment, there was no 'optimism' as Freddie terms it, how could there be amidst so much sadness? Instead I had (and retain) a firm determination to work through anything I wish to explore. As I did throughout the therapy, I will simply relate my story as I perceive it.

I left school at sixteen with no qualifications and by the time I reached twenty I had decided to study for a degree in business studies. This was my first step into recognising the fascinating possibilities available out there in the world beyond me. Emotional development followed later. Although it sometimes was extremely painful, I am thankful beyond words that I went to see Freddie and very much regret not having seen a therapist years earlier.

I learnt how to be in the world by copying my parents' behaviour. This meant adhering to a very controlled, structured and restricted life; opening up to further choices would have necessarily meant leaving something to chance. However, when things are left to chance there is a risk that something different might occur; and if something different would have taken place this would have moved (my parents and/or) me outside the controlled, restricted life we maintained, and we saw any such move as unsafe. Since being open about emotions – i.e. revealing how we felt and thus telling others of our vulnerabilities – involves taking risks, any open discussion of feelings was also excluded from our lives. As a result, at first, I found it very difficult to talk to Freddie. I worried about whether I could trust him not to hurt me if I did 'tell him all about it'.

This says as much about my parents as it does about me since I was copying their behaviour. As the eldest child, I perceived subliminal messages from my parents, which effectively stated that 'we cannot look after you, your siblings, or ourselves, so you must do the caring, you have to look after all of us'. Moreover, not knowing there could be any other way, I accepted this role as a 'good little girl'. I did as I was told. I hid the tremendous pain and sadness of true reality, of not being allowed to be a child, of not freely being allowed to be me. I took on the job of ensuring the safety of my three younger siblings. I felt (and still feel) a tremendous sadness, a loss, an awareness of not being looked after emotionally and thus I became a parent to my parents.

I knew nothing else, and therefore assumed that everyone was like my parents, that no one wanted to know my emotions or me; that everyone would hurt me if I revealed my feelings. Everything had to appear perfect to the outside world, even when so often it was not. If anything – however small – was faulty, I had not just made a mistake, I was just not good at that particular thing, but I was completely useless.

My self-esteem was at rock bottom, it didn't exist; but nobody could be allowed to see that, or that anything was wrong, because everything had to be flawless and if anyone saw that something was wrong then, I argued, 'they wouldn't want to know me, they would reject me and never speak to me again'. So a vicious circle was created as I refused to let people get to know me properly, believing that if they did they would reject me, that they wouldn't want to know someone who was nothing, who was useless. And as a result others were unable to connect with me. Yet, by hiding in this way, by refusing to let others get close to me, I rejected people.

I was very confused and felt totally alone. There will always be a tremendous sadness within me: it is an expression of my lost childhood, it is a wistful sorrowfulness which yearns for the 'lost' warmth and physical and emotional contact my parents never gave me and never will. Hence I feel a deep sorrow that in order to be able to form 'normal' relationships I had to work with a therapist.

Just before my eighth birthday there was a huge family row. I had been required to take the role of peacemaker between my parents and grandmothers, and as usual was successful. I always found this task very stressful. Nevertheless this was a role I accepted. In addition, as a birthday treat I had been allowed to stay up much later than usual that night to watch a film. The next morning I went to the bathroom, to clean my teeth. One moment I was standing in front of the basin, the next thing I was aware of was that I was lying on the lino and felt dizzy and drowsy. My sister found me and shouted for Mum and Dad to come and help, as in her words 'Sophie has fallen down and can't get up'. It must have been terrifying to her six-year-old mind to see the older sister who had always been there to calmly look after and protect her, collapse in that manner.

Mum called the doctor. I was feeling so peculiar that all I could cope with was to lie in bed and sleep. Later that day Mum asked if I would mind if they went out for a while. I told her I did not mind. In fact, I just wanted her out of my hair. Even then, I knew my parents could not look after me, so what was the point in them being around. Again, the sadness overwhelmed me. But on that day so long ago, while I was desperate for some peace and quiet, at the same time having my family leave me alone in the house was a total rejection of my being. I was ill – at that stage we did not know what with – and there might have been a recurrence. If anything was to have happened, there was no one in the house to help me. I was eight years old, confused and shocked. There was no physical pain, but emotionally I was extremely distressed, yet no one offered to discuss how I was with me. So I curled up under the covers to sleep off the physical effects, while my supposed protectors tried to obliterate the problem by discarding me, and hence it.

My collapse was in fact the first of many epileptic seizures. An epileptic seizure is frightening to watch and it is terrifying to know that the individual concerned could unintentionally kill themselves during the course of one – and, of course, terrifying to be that person – especially when you have nearly killed yourself.[1]

Life changed. I do not remember if I ever had fun before that first seizure, but afterwards, having fun was not part of my vocabulary. I became even more defensive and withdrawn than previously, although I did not see it that way. I had no desire to go out socially. I had virtually no friends to bring home after school and rarely received an invitation to visit my peers. There were no in-depth relationships. Boyfriends were virtually non-existent, and most of those I did have were 'not what I wanted in a prospective husband', but they were men whom I could control and thus ensure, what in those days I saw as, my safety through a lack of emotional and physical closeness. I had to keep this physical distance although my own overwhelming sadness persisted and increased.

I had learned that opening up one's vulnerabilities to others is something that is not done. Freddie urged me to challenge this idea. In reality, I needed to turn my ideas upside down, and learn how to tell others about my vulnerabilities and emotions. I learnt that by refusing to tell others of the sadness (and, of course, all other emotions), I had reduced my options, thus making my life miserable. I learnt that it was not just 'their' fault, but also mine; and I learnt that I could take responsibility for doing something about the status quo, that I could choose to change things.

At twenty one, I left my parents' home, moving into a rented flat. Shortly thereafter I met a man, a married man who was about twenty four years older than myself and we started seeing each other. I will call him Ian, but this is not his real name. Communication was difficult because of Ian's married status, but we wrote to each other, he phoned me when his wife and children were safely out of earshot; and from time to time Ian would visit, sometimes staying overnight. However, when he stayed at my flat we always slept separately. Ian in my bed and me in a sleeping bag – in the other room. He wanted sex, but I refused. I was terrified but had no understanding of why. I knew very little about sex beyond the basic mechanics, the anatomical details; I believed sex was intercourse in the missionary position and that it should only take place within marriage. Yet at the same time I felt guilty, as I did let men 'feel me and kiss me all over', and it was pleasurable, but sad, since I 'knew' I should not do that as 'we weren't married and so it wasn't right'. While I let Ian kiss me all over, I would only let him touch me sexually if he kept his trousers on.

One Friday evening, I rushed home from work as Ian was coming to stay that weekend. I was expecting him at eight o'clock. At seven-thirty the phone rang – somehow before I picked up the receiver, I knew it was him and that trouble was brewing. It was indeed Ian, calling to say that he wouldn't be coming to London as his wife had discovered one of my letters, and hence the existence of our 'affair'; and so Ian informed me it was at an end. He sounded very upset, but at the same time was absolutely certain that I was all right and would be able to cope. However, the opposite was true. Although I am able to cope and push myself to continue whatever comes my way, this time coping was beyond me. That night I called the Samaritans, it was the first of many calls I made to them, and with hindsight I know that those calls kept me alive. If the Samaritans had not been there the sadness which frequently led me into extremes of depression would have culminated in suicide.

Shortly after that first call I decided to seek professional help and was referred to Freddie, and we worked together for just over four years. I was usually glad to see him, often extremely relieved to be in my safe haven where I could talk about all the pain and sorrow. On the other hand, there were times when things were different; when Freddie was transformed from a safe rock amidst my sea of sadness and pain into someone who I knew intellectually was trying to help, but who at times was not entirely with me. I refer to some issues of boundaries, which I describe later. I learnt about boundaries from a book I read, and that time I thought that the prerequisite of the right boundary was total consistency and continuity. Despite this, somehow, somewhere, the warmth, support and safe rock won through. During our work together, I frequently sat down at the word processor and wrote about what was going on for me, and I have used some of that material in this manuscript, and include extracts below from these notes. (Author's note: Sophie wrote these notes intending to publish them.)

There was and always had been a terror of sex in Sophie's life. And for that reason she refused to let herself be free and fully open with men. One day the child-woman spoke of a traumatic childhood experience that was part of the ever-repeating cycle in which she found herself stuck. Sophie must have been about five years old on that cataclysmic night. She snapped awake suddenly, somehow knowing she was going to be sick and headed rapidly in the direction of the bathroom. Once the vomiting had ceased, Sophie turned towards her parents' bedroom and knocked on the door. The small child could not tell why it existed or what the need inside her was, but she was instinctively aware that she required some sort of something from her parents. There was no answer to her light tap on the bedroom door, so assuming they were asleep, she opened it.

The sight that met her eyes held her rigid for perhaps thirty seconds, then Sophie snapped the door shut and fled to the warmth and safety of her own bed, where she promptly curled up and hid everything except the very top of her head beneath the covers. What they had been doing she did not know, but the bedclothes were all awry, neither parent had anything on and her father had been lying on top of her mother. A few minutes later her mother arrived to ask what Sophie had wanted. There were no comforting arms extended to console the shaken child, no words of love and warmth – just an inquisition. 'Why was she awake at that hour of the night?; what had she been doing in the hallway?; why had she disturbed her parents?; and what had she wanted from them?' Questions, questions, questions. They drummed into the terrified child.

Sophie explained shakily, whispering her answers, making them as short and succinct as possible. The sickness had completely drained her; and although the child was not aware of it at the time, she was also in a state of shock, and sadness overwhelmed her. It was impossible to voice her feelings, and anyway there was no point in doing so since they would have been rejected. Sophie's mother stood fixedly at the foot of the bed, her face rapidly gaining a bright red complexion, the reason for which perplexed her daughter. She gave her daughter no explanation of what the child had seen. Sophie was left to figure it out on her own.

As a result, I developed the idea that sex is something that should be hidden and not discussed, and from somewhere came the concept that sex is not done except under proper (i.e. married) circumstances. In addition, I came to believe that masturbation is wrong. My work with Freddie changed that. I came to believe that as those who brought me into being – my parents – shut me out, as they didn't and don't want to know me as an emotional being, so I in turn shut out the world which had first created and then abandoned me to rejection and dismissal.

When Freddie and I first met, I believed myself to be a completely useless being, whom nobody wanted to know and who could achieve nothing. That changed, as for the first time in my life I came to know somebody who really accepted me, and who really accepted me to be as I am. It created such a hell of a difference in a very positive way, but as he was the only one in my life like that, it also made what I saw as his 'rejections' – the boundary violations – worse.

The boundary violation was our enforced change of room. I took a week's holiday and on the day I flew home, Freddie left the country for a week's holiday. Prior to this he had warned me that we would have to move room – I hated the idea – and Freddie promised me that 'there would be one last week in the old room, on the lower ground floor, and we would talk about it there' after our holidays. However, he arrived home to find that this would not be possible as the builders had knocked a hole in one of the room's external walls.

I was furious. Part of his job was to provide continuity and as I yelled across the room at him 'you're not doing what you're supposed to do, you're doing the opposite'. Freddie wanted to work in the room I call his study (as it contains floor to ceiling bookshelves and a desk) but I am not comfortable there and refused to do so. We talked about it, covering my feelings of rejection and, of course, the subject of trust. I thought seriously about leaving him, but eventually we compromised and agreed to try working in the lounge area. A fog of sadness and despair descended on me, I was devastated. Freddie had failed me, he had been less than perfect. And according to the value system I employed at that time, anything imperfect was rejected as, by being imperfect, it or they, had rejected me.

More Extracts

She was so low and listless that week, as they recommenced work in the lounge area. Freddie urged her to stay with her feelings. Sophie's voice crept out, dropping from her usual quietly spoken, well-modulated tones into a faint whisper which fell away into silence part way through phrases and sentences.

The therapist was surprised by her reaction, he had a cowering child in front of him. 'Yes', she said, nodding, 'she knew it was childlike. That there was this child in her which screamed and screamed and screamed; and sometimes it retreated into a whispering misery; when she wanted something to happen her way and needed it to be but did not know how to make it come about and had no other resource to make it be that particular way'. Sophie did not know why things were thus, or even what made the child come to the fore. It just was thus.

We discovered in therapy that the child was for me a protector, that when I am wounded or find myself unable to cope I retreat into the child protector. In those days, I could not move my boundaries to accommodate change if it fell outside the limitations I regarded as safe. Whenever I became involved in events outside my self-imposed safe boundaries I simply could not handle the situation and retreated into the child protector. If my safety was threatened I was devastated and slid into a downward spiral of sadness, which frequently became suicidal depression (this pattern was a recurrent theme, which we discussed throughout the therapy). I felt that this move to a different room threatened my safety.

Eventually we compromised and we agreed to continue our work in the lounge area. However, I felt abandoned but not bereft. I wanted him to change his environment to suit me. Throughout our therapeutic relationship I wanted Freddie to be my substitute father and I sought an impossible ideal, a caring parent who never made mistakes, who was always there when he was wanted with exactly what I needed.

During our four years' work, the way I am in the world became more open, more flexible. But still there are restrictions – but then there always will be, since we all need boundaries of some sort. I used to blame Freddie for not challenging me sufficiently, for being too much the father/protector and thus failing to dig out other issues. While he might argue I was equally responsible for raising these issues with him, I would argue that I was not consciously aware they existed. But having said that, I learnt much about myself, and also that therapists are human beings who – like all other human beings – sometimes make mistakes – and hence that therapists who claim that they never make mistakes are dangerous.

My views on masturbation and sexuality changed radically. My fear of sex was closely linked to my refusal to open up in order to connect closely with other human beings. That fear of sex and refusal to enter into close relationships with others is virtually extinct. A small residue remains, based on a few experiences, as occasionally, when I have made myself vulnerable, others involved have hurt me. But usually they do not. The therapy taught me that failure, criticism, and rejection does not automatically ensue from moving boundaries and taking risks, but that in fact flexibility has the opposite effect, as it makes room for other options, options which previously were excluded by rigid, fixed, and hence restrictive boundaries. My life became more open, more forward looking, as more choices became possible, while my all too frequent bouts of depression and sadness dissipated. Sometimes the sadness still affects me. But now I have the tools with which to halt the sadness and that formerly repetitive spiral of depression.

CONCLUSION

When we speak of sadness, we have to remember that each emotion interacts with other emotions. That was so with Sophie. Her sadness had predominated the therapy but it had also intrinsically correlated with anger, jealousy, and other emotions. I was surprised that a year ago she had yet again a seizure, despite the fact that they appeared to have totally disappeared when our therapy course ended. This was a sad reminder for Sophie of the ever lasting effect of her predicament.

There were two aspects of the therapy where our perception differed to some degree. I had not felt fully the deep suffering that Sophie disclosed about the change of the consulting room. I knew that it was difficult for her and I also realised that her decision to stay or leave was often 'on a knife edge'. Now, I realise that the deep-seated fear of abandonment and loneliness was much more ingrained then I was able to identify with at the time. Opposed to this, I apprehended a more profound fear and hopelessness in her sexual issues than, according to her chronicle, was Sophie's perception of it at the time.

The mindfulness of our 'world-view' in itself facilitates the creation of human bond between therapists and clients. In other words, the awareness and the acknowledgement of the universality of human destiny, in the face of the givens of the world, furthers the empathic relationship. At the same time, however, we have to acknowledge that beyond the universality of the 'givens' there exists a vast and infinite diversity in human behaviour. This does not only manifest itself in each individual's behaviour, but also in the mode and the quality of the perception of the emotions that each of us experiences. This refers not only to the differences between individuals but also between the differences that individual's experience at different times. This was clearly demonstrated in the differences between Sophie's and my perceptions of her pain and her own emotional experiences. All in all, however, I felt that Sophie had become aware of her world-view and even after therapy experienced many insights. I feel that the therapy had given her some of an impetus for her further insights and development.

NOTE

1. If you do see someone having an epileptic seizure, they may move about. Do not try to physically restrain them in any way, and do not put anything in their mouth. Instead, stay with them, but try to keep them away from any dangers, i.e. sharp knives, gas flames. If the seizure continues for more than five minutes call a doctor. Further information about epilepsy may be obtained from the National Society for Epilepsy on 01494-601300 or the British Epilepsy Association on 0113-243-9393.

7

Shame

Shame is an emotion which is intrinsically interlinked with guilt. It is true that emotions usually overlap with each other, as can be seen from examples described in other chapters. Yet, shame and guilt are so much intertwined with each other that one cannot detect one without the other. When I am ashamed of something I also experience guilt about doing something wrong because in my perception I did not fulfil my own expectations.

In addition, shame has an essential importance for me and for my therapeutic encounters. I experience a direct and almost visceral connection between guilt, shame and our value systems. Shame reveals my own culturally imposed moral imperatives, as well as those of my clients. That is, the values which my clients and I accept as basic requirements for approval by others and ourselves.

For example, in my early childhood between the ages of seven and eight I was taught, or rather indoctrinated with the idea, that touching my genitals was forbidden. Needless to say, at that age, I accepted that dictum without question. In relation to this, an image in which I am standing in the middle of the photograph between dozens of my peers frequently appeared in my mind. My governess had cut out an oblong slice from the middle of the photo in order to obliterate the shame of touching my genitals with one of my hands. There is no need to elaborate on my struggle to shake off the imperative that in order to be a good person one must not touch one's genitals. But the awareness of this shame and the guilt disclosed an aspect of my world-view in exactly the same manner as Cherry, one of my ex-clients, disclosed her shame and world-view – although in a different context, as will be seen in the next section of this chapter.

CHERRY

Cherry's presenting problem centred on her perception of her excessive weight. In the course of the early part of the therapy, she had become aware that she would either have to accept herself the way she was or do something about it. She decided to take action about her condition and the option she had chosen was to change her body. Regular visits to a gym had now became her aim, although this was easier said than done.

Early on in the therapy, Cherry recalled an experience that helped her understand some of her problems. 'I began my journey to the gym quite cheerfully and looked forward to a new experience. As I approached the street, however, it suddenly dawned on me that I had not properly thought the situation through. I would have to undress and expose my body to others in the dressing room and subsequently in the gym; this in itself raised an immediate alarm in me. How would I undress if someone was watching? The closer I got to my destination the more anxious I became. As I walked, I began to visualise increasingly the scene of my fears. I saw myself gradually undressing and others observing my bottom. This thought alone made me almost turn round and run home. I succeeded in overcoming my fear by sheer will power and I dragged myself to the premises. I was shown to the dressing room and as each layer of clothing came off, so my dread increased. Suddenly I found myself at the entrance of the gym. The door was slightly ajar. I glanced inside, and then a sudden feeling of panic struck me. My legs trembled, my heart pounded and I suddenly found myself unable to move an inch. I froze completely, lost my sense of where and who I was and then unexpectedly I felt a gentle touch on my shoulder. Suddenly I was alert and felt as if I had just awoken from a dream. The male gym instructor was kindly and cautiously guiding me to the exercise room.' This image of Cherry was profoundly imprinted on my mind and followed the therapy as a metaphor and a guiding light.

Therapy.

The first time I saw Cherry was when she arrived for our introductory session. She had a charming and handsome face, although she was somewhat overweight with largish hips. The fact that I noticed all this at once was, I believe, due to her postural behaviour. I surmised that this gave away her desire to conceal her physical being. Her gaze was downwards and her shoulders stooped, and this made her look a lot smaller than she was. Without naming the person, she said that one of my ex-clients, who had similar problems, had referred her to me.

Even before we discussed our contract, Cherry had no difficulty whatsoever in telling me about some of her problems. Throughout her life, she had done all she could to reduce her weight drastically. She went to Weight Watchers, counselling; she saw a psychiatrist; and now it seemed there was nothing else she could do.

Cherry was born in London where she lived happily with her parents and her sister – at least this was her recollection. Her sister was three years older, which seemed a great deal for Cherry at such a young age. She looked up to her sister because after all she was living a much 'freer' life than Cherry. In her perception this 'clever and desirable adult' could go out when she wanted, while her little sister had to stay at home.

The family's idyllic and peaceful existence had been suddenly disrupted. She was around eight years old when her father's business collapsed. From a cheerful, optimistic and well-to-do man, her father changed into a worried, dispirited and introverted person. Cherry spoke with great melancholy about this transformation in her family life, as if her whole happiness had been shattered by this 'catastrophe'. She said that from then onwards her father could not give her the attention and care she had previously enjoyed.

This recollection lasted for about fifteen minutes and I then asked her 'Cherry, could you recall one of those happy moments, which you spoke of?' It took her quite a while to gather her thoughts and to recount an episode that had made a deep impression. She was seven years old when she spent a holiday on the South Coast with her family. This was a happy memory for her, as everything was peaceful and free. She enjoyed her father's attention and his loving and caring feelings towards her. She particularly remembered a sunny day when she was swimming with her father and felt his warmth towards her. She felt not only secure, but also very happy. The happiness was mixed with sadness in this story, and her nostalgic desire to return to this happy and secure place was very moving for me. I sensed this could have been her lost paradise, which might become a major theme in the therapy.

We proceeded with a therapy course that consisted initially of twelve sessions and one review session. In the event we renegotiated her therapeutic needs and agreed on another module of twelve sessions. It transpired in the early part of the therapy that her issues centred on food, bingeing, and her body, but she also experienced great difficulties in forming intimate relationships. When I asked her what was her expectation of the therapy, Cherry was quite clear in her aim to be able to form intimate relationships. In one of the sessions, she detailed the immense pain she had felt that morning when she had to face another meaningless day of joyless work and without a significant relationship to look forward to. 'What was there to live for?' She spoke of her loneliness and fears of facing the world. She accepted the fact that living with her sister and even knowing people from work gave her the opportunity to socialise. All this were vastly overshadowed, however, by her inexorable drive to engage only in close relationships.

I felt that it was now the appropriate time for Cherry to explore those feelings of happiness and joy, before that inauspicious time when her world 'crumbled' as in her perception everything changed after her father's business difficulties. I prompted Cherry to investigate that joy of swimming with her father, happily and carelessly, which she missed so much. Cherry sobbed and wondered how could she feel happy with her 'hateful' large bottom, and detestable figure. How could others accept her? She then unburdened herself with a story from her teenage years. After her father's mood change, she sensed that she had lost her place of importance at home. Home was a gloomy place; her sister went her own way. Her father was totally absorbed in his business worries, and her mother was preoccupied with looking after her father. There was, in her perception, nobody to listen to her pain and her problems. By the time she was eleven, food had become her only solace. From her early times at school to the beginning of her college days, she felt excluded from her peers. She was fat with large hips and in her view there was not the slightest chance, that she could be part of the 'normal' world – she felt an outsider wherever she went. Her continuous escape from the world's woes was eating, and more eating, really her only joy. In spite of those adversities, she achieved good enough marks in her examinations to obtain a place at college. There, she began to socialise, although it took supreme effort.

I challenged Cherry by saying: 'you had to have something special, will power, and much else, to perform in the midst of your torments'. She accepted the fact that she possessed a great deal of energy and strength to survive and function. She spoke of her efforts to become the centre of attention and a leader in her social environment, both at college and at work. How could she do that, I prompted? She must have needed superhuman energy to do that and to conceal her inner weakness. She felt that she had to hide her looks with lots of loose clothing and make-up so that people would not discover what was underneath. Through sheer willpower, she succeeded in dieting and losing weight in her early twenties. She felt better, but she still found it impossible to have an intimate relationship.

Already, early in the sessions, I felt that Cherry was totally committed to the therapy. I was naturally pleased, as this complied with our verbal contract. We had both committed ourselves whole-heartedly to the therapy. Yet I also felt that through this commitment Cherry put enormous pressure on herself and on the therapeutic process. She wanted to achieve her goal wholly within the agreed period of time. She pushed herself and I felt pressurised as well. The positive effect of this situation was that the sessions became extremely intensive. There was, however, a negative side to it, in that I had to be extremely careful to suspend my wish to find an instant cure for her. I felt great empathy with Cherry, almost to the extent that I identified with her suffering: her feeling of pain: a helpless undervalued person, alone, meaningless, and without self-esteem. I became fully aware in the therapeutic sessions that I had to 'tune out' as I needed to prompt Cherry to explore and challenge her ambivalence and contradictions.

I mused what it might be that made Cherry's beliefs about her looks so rigid and caused her withdrawal from any male relationship. What made her whole being dependent on one assumption, that to be 'somebody' she had to have a certain body? I wanted Cherry to explore how her belief systems influenced her lifestyle. Until now, she had focused on the absence of sexual relationships, which she longed for. She was thirty three and had never had a genuinely intimate relationship. We were, by now, in the middle of the first module of the therapy. She gradually learned that, as she was terrified to let anyone see her 'large bottom' or her 'detested' body, she could never fulfil a desired relationship with a man. We then discussed how this issue effected her work. She comprehended how work was meaningless for her. She simply regarded it as a necessary evil, and it brought no pleasure for her.

While exploring her feelings about work, we discovered the immense pressure she brought on herself to appear physically and mentally 'correct'. She did not want people to see through her psyche, and was desperate that her large bottom and 'inferior' being must not be discovered. She became very skilful at masking her inner feelings so that her employment did not suffer. She did become very good at her job and a leading light in her social life. All this was achieved, however, at the expense of tremendous exhaustion and, sadly, without much pleasure. The large bottom had intruded in all spheres of life: her personal, sexual, and working relationships, but most of all in her relationship with herself.

In one session in the middle of the first module, she described her relationship with men. Kissing and caressing had been as far as she would go in her sexual relationships. She was so insecure about her body that she could not undress herself, though with determination and will power, she had slept with some of her partners. I urged her to relate an example. She vividly spoke of an encounter in bed with her clothes on. On this occasion, she came very close to actually undressing. Her desolate fear that her partner would see her naked body, however, was too great and she could not undress.

I asked her how she really felt then. She found that it was close to impossible for her to contemplate how she actually felt in that situation. She understood how her self-esteem had totally depended on her 'despised' body especially her bottom. She was 'lost', and in her helpless state she sobbed voicelessly.

As always, I approached her with empathy. I hypothesised and asked her to imagine a situation when despite her perception of her 'gross' and ugly body, she would still find a blissfully happy relationship with a partner. How would that feel? She responded spontaneously and without hesitation, 'as long as I have this figure, this bottom, it would not mean a thing to me'.

During this session it became abundantly clear to both of us that her attitude towards her 'disgusting' body overwhelmed any other feeling. We both understood at this stage that the problem was not only her relationships with others, but that it lay within herself. I, therefore, asked Cherry if she could find any other meaning in her life. She acknowledged that she had a totally rigid image of her body, creating her inner problem. For her, the only way to become 'somebody' was to be slim, with a well-proportioned body. Moreover, it would not have mattered a whit, if a 'partner' had greatly admired her looks and loved her. She would still have despised herself, as that inferior being with the large bottom. I had considerable difficulty in challenging her to view positive aspects of her life. In my opinion, her positive worth was considerable, but it had still taken us until the seventh session to be able to explore this. She had charm, a pleasant face, she was intelligent, had considerable will power, and an empathic ability to relate to people. In objective terms, therefore, she should have had many meanings to her life, other than her preoccupation with her body. On a voluntary basis, Cherry successfully worked with people with Alzheimer's disease. She made friends with over-weight people who, despite their weight problems, were self-confident. However, all these positive aspects of her life were not enough for Cherry and she continued to sob. 'The mind knows, but the body cannot accept it'. She said she could not reject the notion of shame for being an obese person.

I questioned Cherry about the present. 'How would you feel if you undressed here, as metaphorically you have undressed already?' She replied without hesitation 'I could trust you as a professional. I know I can tell all without the fear of you becoming judgmental'. I asked her if she could transpose this position, to an 'external' situa-tion. 'That is what I need to do, but I cannot', she said firmly. She continued to torment herself, but blamed her parents and her envi-ronment for not having been able to acquire the necessary know-how to experiment with sex, like most of her peers had done. 'I learned only at the age of twenty eight, from my sister, what mas-turbation was'. In the event, this did not give her total satisfaction, either.

In one of the sessions, well into the second half of the module, Cherry became desperate and very angry with me. She wanted to know why her thoughts had been so confused. She felt that I should have been able to clarify what was going on in her mind. I fastened on to her anger so that we could explore it thoroughly. She was angry with me as well as with herself for not being able to beget some joy in her life. I again challenged her to look back to when she was eight years old, and remember the joy she had felt when swimming with her father. Was there nothing left of this feeling now? Cherry gradually began to chal-lenge herself. She remembered the joy of helping Alzheimer's patients, the gladness at being with her sister and many other happy relation-ships, all these despite her perceived difficulties. Finally, she also conceded that she had satisfaction from our therapeutic sessions.

By the following session her mood had visibly changed. Cherry had made some important decisions, principally that she had to change her job. She remembered a man she liked who gave her confi-dence. They had met during her work with Alzheimer's patients. A good session I thought, but at once I warned myself of possible sur-prises to come.

The following session Cherry, yet again, arrived in a desperate state. She had seen a man at a nearby building site who, she felt certain, had ridiculed her body. She construed even a cursory look from a stranger as an insult. Once again, she was back to bingeing. We explored this and Cherry insisted it was her only real joy, although she knew that she felt unhappy with her body.

Nearing the end of the first module, Cherry understood her sedimented world-view. She recognised her rigid value system, her low self-esteem, her withdrawal from relationships, and she understood her bingeing. She had learned how bingeing was her strategy for survival. Most important of all, she also accepted the fact that it depended on her attitude whether there would be a change in her lifestyle. Could she accept herself with all her positive and negative aspects and change her rigid world-view? This, in turn, could change her general behaviour and mood. I continued to encourage Cherry, in preparation for the end of the therapy, to keep challenging her negative outlook.

In the ninth session, Cherry appeared chirpy. All her news was good news. She had left her job for a marvellous new one. She had even succeeded in speaking with one of her close friends about her shame. I felt this might be the right time to ask her what would happen if for some reason the therapy had to end that day. Could she contemplate anything positive or indeed negative to take with her from our encounters? Did she get any impetus from our nine sessions for further exploration? Cherry felt that she now approached both her work and her life in general from a somewhat different perspective than before. But she still could not accept her overweight body. In this respect, nothing much had changed. She still felt the need to wear loose clothing and a lot of make-up to 'mask' her looks as much as possible. In the twelfth session, we decided on an additional module of twelve sessions. The main reason for this was that although Cherry felt by now she understood how she functioned, she still needed deeper insight before she felt strong enough to fend for herself.

The Second Module

At the start of the second module, Cherry decided that she and no one else would make the changes she wanted to make in her life. Cherry realised that her attitude to her inner-self was based on her value system, that she still could not accept herself. She clearly grasped her manifold choices. Nevertheless, she had chosen to work on her body. She decided to frequent a gym and take Alexander Technique lessons.

Cherry wanted to write an assessment of herself and brought to the therapy her notes for discussion. One of the main features in her notes was her dependence on food. She wrote 'I enjoy it, it gives me something to look forward to. Nevertheless, why? Just for survival'. She needed joy in her life, but food was the only source of joy. I asked her what she felt when bingeing, when she put food into her mouth. She could not resist that joy. After all what else did she have in her life. She worked on the self-control she so badly needed, but she could not exert it as far as food was concerned. Not even for her intimate relationships, or love, had she been able to contemplate controlling her compulsion to eat, however necessary it was. Session after session our discussions centred on this compulsion. Yet her bingeing continued. Despite all her difficulties, some changes began to take place. She now felt extremely happy about her job, and there were incidents of intimate exchanges with friends. She worked hard to be at the centre of attention.

Cherry arrived greatly disturbed to one of the sessions in the middle of the second module. She had woken up that morning again feeling that the only meaning in life was her body. We deliberated about the things that were still important in her life. We spoke about her work with patients with Alzheimer's syndrome and we spoke about our therapeutic relationship. While she liked all these things, they had not mattered. Her 'head' could not accept her body and her body could not accept her 'head'.

I argued with myself whether a Gestalt role-playing exercise might be appropriate. While I was tempted, I considered that it might be too artificial in the present situation. I then spontaneously decided to go ahead with it and explained the exercise to Cherry. It consisted of two chairs, one for her and one to remain empty. I asked her to talk to the empty chair and believe it represented her body, and to do so in the present tense and in the first person. Without any hesitation, she embraced the experiment and role-played very well. She demanded to know from her body, first of all, why could she not accept herself as she was? Her body posed similar questions to her 'other' self. This dialogue carried on for some fifteen minutes when I asked Cherry's body to ask Cherry's mind what it was it wanted from her and vice versa.

I assumed that this exercise really made an impression on Cherry. Everything that she already knew became even clearer to her. Indeed, in the week after she began to speak about her body and mental conception in an encouraging way. I thought that perhaps she was now ready to try and change her general attitude. Cherry spoke of a bulimic friend of hers. She had suggested to her friend that it was possible to change her behaviour pattern, which reflected encouragingly on her own changing attitude. She was happy with her work and her new promotion at the office. She had fruitful discussions with her parents, which were made easier as Cherry gradually understood her father's vulnerabilities.

Overall, as we approached the end of the therapy, Cherry became increasingly optimistic. This did not mean there were no setbacks. In one of the sessions, she reverted to her depressive mood and spoke about a difficult morning. She wanted to skip the subject. I persisted, since after all she was here to discuss her difficulties. She then explained how the previous night and that morning she had yet again felt how meaningless her life really was. She was devoid of positive desires or goals. There was just her and nobody else there to help her in her misery.

I inadvertently challenged her to explore whether there really was nobody there for her. The moment I made the intervention I regretted it, as I immediately felt very uncomfortable with my remark. She said that nobody but nobody could understand her pain. I felt immense empathy with her and understood how right she was. I explained that I understood her at that moment, though I could not totally experience her feeling of pain. I suggested that she should not try to suppress the feeling of pain, rather to stay with it. There was a long silence. She had tears in her eyes and said that 'not being would have been better then being' and wept. After a further long silence, I asked her how she felt now. 'Relieved', she answered.

In the next session we debated the possibility of trusting other people like she trusted the therapy. If this were possible, she could be more open and enjoy other relationships. She challenged herself and recounted a story of meeting a very kind stranger on one of her visits to a Far Eastern country. There was an immediate resonance between them. She was in an unfamiliar place and agreed to follow her new partner to his room. He was intelligent, gentle and she took a liking to him immediately. This one time, her bodily 'shame' did not matter. In all his approaches, he guided her gently. She described a scene, with immense emotion, where she had succeeded with the help of her strong willpower to come out of the bathroom undressed, with only her knickers on. Her new partner patiently and delicately persuaded her, and she agreed, to have oral sex with him. Cherry's mood, in telling this story had become 'lighter'. After all the situation was amusing, especially when her partner asked 'How can I do that with your nickers on?' I challenged her by asking: 'When you had your new friend guiding you, or the gym instructor had his guiding hand on you, were you able to forget your shame?' Cherry said spontaneously 'That is what happens here, between you and me'. During the next session, she retold a story from the office. A colleague at work had invited her via the Intranet. She was hesitant, but accepted the invitation. However, one week went by and there was no word from him. That was the moment when she decided to take the initiative and ring him. 'Does it take so long for you to decide?' she asked. They agreed on the time and spent a very pleasant evening together. They made an arrangement to spend Christmas together.

We approached the end of the second module and Cherry was hesitant about the ending. She asked herself what could she get out of further therapy. After all, she knew already that her shame and self-esteem hinged on her self-imposed value that she could not be accepted as a person unless she reduced her weight. She also acknowledged the fact that it was possible to shake up her rigid belief system. Yet, although many things had changed, she was also aware of the fact that her rigid sedimentation about her body would creep back periodically. Cherry felt that while she could function normally in her life she was not certain how she would be without therapy when and if she regressed into her low state. We agreed that during the last review session we would jointly decide whether she would need another module of therapy and, if so, what would be the duration.

Cherry arrived at our last review session in a serene and optimistic mood. She appeared more feminine in her choice of clothing and her posture had changed to an upright position. Her mood was bright and she felt that she could now accept herself as she was. She had been to a few parties and felt unusually comfortable. She had not cared whether they would accept her body, as she was there to enjoy herself. She thought she might have acquired sufficient confidence to deal with her issues herself.

I felt uneasy about what I believed was an over-buoyant mood. I was familiar enough with such mood changes not to be entirely comfortable with Cherry's assessment. I had experienced how such moods could soon change and be transformed into loneliness and isolation. She asked me whether I agreed with her and what I thought about not embarking on another therapeutic module. While I agreed that she had changed considerably in her beliefs and behaviour, and that especially in the latter part of the therapy she had been able to deal with her own issues between the therapy sessions, I brought to her attention the fact that her low self-esteem might return from time to time and that she would have to explore herself. I was confident that she was able and strong enough to find new meanings in her life. Furthermore, after a certain time she could always call me if she needed me.

As time progressed, the mood in the session became more solemn and Cherry began to record her last meeting with her parents. On the one hand, she could feel very hard and angry towards her parents. On the other hand, she felt guilty about her adverse emotions and forced herself to be as nice as possible to them. The fact remained that Cherry felt totally disregarded by her father, while her mother, it seemed to her, had stood by with neglectful equanimity. Cherry was able to express her strong anger towards her father. She accused him of an inability to stay with her for one moment and listen to her problems and her torments. On the occasion they had last met, she spoke on the telephone to her mother asking her for advice. When her father was called to the telephone, he flatly refused to be involved. I encouraged her to study and analyse her anger. She soon became conscious that her father's refusal to listen to her meant a total rejection, an annihilation of her being. This in turn threw her into a helpless isolated place with no self-esteem. I left Cherry to contemplate that for a while, when I asked her whether she could look at and explore her father's emotional precepts.

When Cherry's anger subsided, she was able gradually to rectify her father's image in his naked vulnerable state. She saw her father, the Jewish immigrant, arriving in this country without any material or other means, struggling to survive and to bring up his family. Cherry further saw her father as a person whose only aspiration in life was to acquire material means to make his family happy. Cherry thought that her father's neglect was the result of his vulnerability. It suddenly dawned on Cherry that her father's sudden debacle must have badly dented his pride and self-respect. This and the threat of not being able to provide his family with everything they were used to, must have thrown her father into a lonely place of isolation and low self-esteem – Cherry was so very familiar with this place. She argued and finally realised that her father's rigid belief that he could only make his family happy with material goods was very similar, although in a different way, to her own rigid value that to be happy you must have small buttocks.

Finally, Cherry explored, as we had done many times before, other possibilities for her to create meaning in her life. We again scrutinised her effectiveness and capacities in her life. She was aware from our innumerable discussions of her capacity to listen. She knew that she had a charming and pleasant face, and acknowledged her ability to help people. This was proven to her by her successful voluntary work with individuals with Alzheimer disease. Then, surprisingly, Cherry decided to explore the possibility of enrolling in an evening class to learn counselling. This was a total surprise to me, as she had never mentioned this possibility before.

We parted with a very warm handshake.

Supervision

This section of the book will describe two cases and their supervision. The purpose is to illustrate the process of supervision and how focusing on emotions assists supervisees with understanding their own and their client's world-views.

In order to acquaint readers with the process of supervision, I will briefly outline how I see the function of supervision in counselling and in psychotherapy. The term supervision as applied to supervising trainee and qualified therapists and counsellors is somewhat inappropriate. The word supervision in ordinary language connotes an activity when one individual oversees another's work – the supervisor is in authority whilst the supervisee accepts instructions. This implies an authoritarian relationship.

Supervision, however, is not intended to be like that in most therapeutic models. According to the British Association of Counselling's Code of Ethics, the function of supervision is to monitor, develop and support individuals to grow in their helping or counselling role. This does not exactly mean a relationship where the supervisor is the boss and the trainee must comply. Admittedly, there are as many approaches to supervision as there are different therapeutic orientations. However, while these differences influence the way the term is understood, there is a consensus between counsellors and psychotherapists that supervision is an activity aimed at enhancing supervisees' skills and their understanding of the practice of counselling or psychotherapy.

The root of supervision goes back to Sigmund Freud and started in 1902 when a number of young doctors established a circle around him to learn practising and 'spreading' psychoanalysis. This has since moved from informal learning to a training structure that provides the basic components used in most current training programmes. In 1925, an international training commission was established to formalise requirements for supervision (Page and Wosket:1994). This comprised supervising, teaching and personal analysis. Since then

118

supervision has undergone a rapid evolution. Nowadays supervision takes place to train and monitor counsellors, psychotherapists and trainee practitioners. Universities, training organisations, and institutions that accredit counsellors and psychotherapists require as part of training a specified number of hours supervised practice with clients. There are three types of supervision: those which are conducted in groups; those carried out person to person (one to one); and those which are between experienced therapists, called co- or peer supervision.

I have been in a fortunate position that for many years I have had the opportunity to supervise in colleges, institutions, and in private practice both trainees and experienced counsellors and therapists. This experience has taught me that the term 'supervision' in itself might impede successful training because it can increase the possible feeling of defensiveness of the supervisees. Supervisees inevitably try to present their cases with what in their perception is 'good therapy'. When they feel criticised, emotion surges and a resistance to listening develops. Sometimes supervisors cannot resist having an attitude of superiority. This is evidently counterproductive, even if merely manifested in a paternalistic manner.

I feel that the best way one can evaluate how supervisees deal with their clients is through their behaviour and their emotions in the supervision session itself. Defences and resistance to feedback are an indication of difficulties. After all, therapists are often subject to fierce criticisms by clients. In any supervision session when emotions and feelings are evoked in such a way, these need to be analysed. The question then arises: to what extent should supervision overlap psychotherapy, that is to say how far can the supervisee be analysed in supervision?

In order to alleviate these situations, I always discuss with groups or individuals the process between us. I also encourage them to present their problems and failures, disclosing their vulnerabilities as well as their successes. I consider it a strength and not a weakness if we are able to become aware of our emotions and overcome the desire to protect our self-esteem. My role in supervision is mainly to listen, empathetically prompt and explain my way of working and the assumptions behind it.

If a supervisee can reveal his or her vulnerability and look at their own world-view, they will be able to establish an empathic relationship with their clients and in turn prompt them to reveal their world-view and challenge their discrepancies. This, after all, is what therapy is about.

The following sections will discuss the emotion of joy, working in one to one supervision with a drama therapist. This will be followed by a discussion about the love hate paradox in the context of co-supervision.

8
Joy

Joy and happiness are connected words, yet they have two different connotations. Joy refers to an acutely intense reaction, whereas happiness is a state of well-being, harmony, an equilibrium that lasts longer. While joy can be attributed to specific events, happiness is more a way we evaluate our life in general. Nonetheless, joy is connected with happiness as it contributes to it. Happiness and joy have to be distinguished from sensory pleasures, such as eating, taste and touch. Even these in conjunction with others can overlap and give the feeling of joy and happiness. Many authors see joy, in van Deurzen-Smith's words, as the 'summum bonum' (1997:245), the highest good. Joy is in itself the highest 'good' to which we aspire. Real joy for me increases my capacity to appreciate the world, the closeness of beauty and goodness. I believe, like Schulz, Maslow, and Rogers, that openness and honesty are essential ingredients for experiencing joy and happiness (1991:144). When I am happy and joyful, my posture and nervous system express this explicitly and I am closer and more open to others and the world.

Yet, happiness and joy need not always be positive. Bernard Shaw wrote 'But a lifetime of happiness! No man alive could bare it: it would be hell on earth' (1905/1963:527). Joy can be an outright negative emotion. If joy is mastery of other people or triumph over them, then there must be a psychological problem involved. Surely, the Nazis' joy at torturing and killing innumerable people could not be classified as a positive emotion. This brings me to another aspect of joy, namely schadenfreude. This is joy about other people's misfortunes. What kind of joy is it when Milosevic, the Serbian dictator, gloats about his victory, 'ethnically cleansing' thousands of people. This is his schadenfreude over his opponents. I was quite puzzled that in my extensive research about emotions, I have not been able to find any theory and classification of schadenfreude.

When I speak of the negativity of happiness, inevitably Richard P. Bentall's imaginative, though bizarre, article on happiness springs to mind. While one cannot take Bentall's article too literally, it neverthe-less brings to mind many worthwhile thoughts. In 'A Proposal to Classify Happiness as a Psychiatric Disorder', he suggests that happi-ness can be appraised as a psychiatric disorder. He argues that if one takes socially unacceptable behaviour as the criteria for a mental dis-order, then happiness is irrational 'because happiness often results in action which fails to realise manifest goals, and which therefore decreases the happy person's expected utilities' (1992:96). He argues that 'irrationality may be demonstrated by the detection of cognitive deficits and distortions of one sort or another' (1992:97). Happiness has no goals and it is therefore irrational. Bentall further postulates: 'it has been shown that happy people in comparison to people who are miserable or depressed, are impaired when they retrieve negative events from long term memory' (ibid). In short, he argues that there is a prima facie case for classifying happiness as a psychiatric disorder, suitable for inclusion in future editions of DSM IV (American Diagnostic and Statistical Manual of Mental Disorders).

In therapy, joy and happiness are at least as important as negative emotions. This is often contrary to the popular belief that therapy is only about despair, depression and other negative feelings. Indeed, joy can express and reveal clients' world-view as well as any other emotion. In most sessions, if there is an opportunity, I try to evoke a moment of happiness and joy and I ask my clients to stay with that feeling. When I challenge clients, I also try to do this positively by pointing out their strengths and positive aspects of their life. In this process, clients often connect with negative emotions. In a combina-tion of all these, clients explore their world-view and challenge their discrepancies. Because joy increases one's capacity to appreciate others and the world, it also creates a bond and a oneness with others. In this exploration in therapy, clients usually link or juxtapose happi-ness with their negative experiences like despair and loneliness.

A striking example of joy and despair in my own experience occurred in a totally unexpected way when a joyful moment left a very deep impression on my life. One of my daughters, who I had not seen for some time, visited me with her husband and a friend. One evening, what started out as a normal, predictable conversation devel-oped into an argument between my daughter and myself. As the discussion became more and more intense, my daughter accused me of not being interested in her and not caring for her. 'You are only interested in your own agenda and your own life'. Slowly but surely both our tempers rose. I felt at that moment that I had given her so much love, care, and devotion in my life, yet she ignored me and belittled me.

My temper grew as I thought she was trying to denigrate me in front of her husband and friend. I asked her if she had come to visit me to 'disown' me. Then, I suddenly noticed that her chin started to quiver. I knew this was a sign that she was about to cry, conveying her vulnerability and deep pain. I suddenly realised that I was full of anger and many other emotions and thus had lost the capacity to see her vulnerability. My anger, I then saw, was about my injured self-esteem: I could only protect my superiority with outbursts of anger. Indeed, I feared my inadequacy would be revealed, namely that I was just a weak person who was unable to maintain the control of being a good paterfamilias with authority. This was what my self-imposed moral value system dictated to me.

By the time I realised all this, it was too late. She had put her coat on and left the room with her chin still quivering. For half an hour, I was in total despair and wished that the earth would open and swallow me. The only solace I had was the empathic total silence between my daughter's husband, the friend, and myself. After half an hour, my daughter reappeared and we both exited to the kitchen embraced and wept. We both revealed our vulnerabilities and it reacquainted me with my real world-view. I was filled with joy.

Claire Schrader wrote the case study that follows this introduction. I knew Claire by reputation only and I attended one of her workshops. It was, therefore a pleasure for me when she asked for a one to one supervision course. She is a drama therapist, and I had not supervised anybody from this orientation before. She is well-respected in the profession. The problem she presented was that one of her clients had prematurely left her therapy, and this especially interested me.

At first, we both experienced some difficulty in understanding each other's theoretical orientation. I found it remarkable, however, that by the end of four sessions Claire arrived at an insight into the way I work, and of its fundamental existential underpinning. I have always worked with dreams and occasionally with art therapy. I have found that art brings emotions to the surface very quickly. I have to acknowledge that Claire's drama therapy could induce in a very short time the kind of intense primal and unexpurgated emotions that are needed for the exploration of one's world-view. Claire and I both agreed to further our experience by researching methods and skills for an amalgamation of ideas.

There now follows Claire's chronicle of Emma's case in the context of our supervision sessions.

Drama Therapy

I am a drama therapist. I sought the help of Freddie Strasser to supervise the case of Emma, a twenty-six-year-old dancer who came to me for individual drama therapy on a friend's recommendation, in order to explore her anger. Emma left the therapy prematurely, and I hoped the existential supervision would provide new insight into her case.

The room I work in is large enough for both of us to move around freely. The form of each session takes a ritual structure with a clear beginning, middle, and end.

The drama therapy sessions involved using the symbols and metaphors of a story as a means of exploring the theatre of Emma's inner self. We worked in a theatrical and physical way in which Emma expressed herself through her voice and body, often making use of non-verbal language and ritual to work through issues.

At the beginning, we sat on the floor on a gold cloth in a corner which was identified as the place where we could discuss relevant issues. When it became clear what was going to be the theme of the session, we moved off the gold cloth into the body of the room. There Emma could explore ways of expressing herself creatively through movement, story or creative play. A number of materials were available for her to use. These included a large bag of brightly coloured cloths, a boxful of hats and props and a variety of percussion instruments. There were also puppets, drawing materials, mask-making materials and playdoh, which would be used in any way Emma chose to express an aspect of the story.

An important part of the session was the deroleing process in which Emma left behind the character and the imaginative world she had created and returned to herself and her own reality. Often this involved clearing any objects, furniture, or pieces of cloth that she had used as a costume or to create this world. If the session had been very emotional, she might have to shake out her body and literally shake out the character.

At the end of the session, we returned to the gold cloth in order to reflect on the material Emma had explored. In this part of the session,

Emma was able to comment on the emotions she had experienced and the meaning the metaphors of the drama had for her. Often, if Emma had not been able to make sense of them at the time, she would gain more insight in the time between sessions, and would bring this back for discussion.

In each drama therapy session, Emma created and worked through parts of a story. Through the story, Emma revealed herself to me in terms her values and the issues she was wrestling with. The therapy was in her physical and imaginative exploration of the story and the insights she gained through its telling. But more importantly, because working with the story also involved engaging with archetypes, symbols and the language of the unconscious, there were always elements that could never be reduced to rational explanation.

Emma

Emma had recently returned to London with her boyfriend after a period of working in the provinces, in order to establish her career in the capital. What I noticed first about Emma was her physical beauty and her very apparent sexuality, which was masked by unattractive clothing. We struck up an immediate rapport. I saw in Emma's use of appeasing expressions and gestures, a mirror of my own approval-seeking strategies. I had the sense that Emma was apologising for her physical attributes.

In our first session, Emma had reviewed her intention to work on anger and said that she was looking for guidance. I explained that this was not my role but that she would find her own answers in what she explored. Emma went on to clarify that she was looking to find balance and harmony within herself. Since she had limited resources, (she was out of work at the time) we agreed on ten sessions with the proviso that this might need to be extended if the work stirred up material that needed to be integrated further.

Because Emma was a dancer, she was very comfortable with using her body and expressed it in a very free way. There was a sense of unreserved freedom and joy in the way she engaged with the drama therapy session as if this was an opportunity she had been seeking for some time.

I introduced Emma to the Hero's Journey, which would provide the framework for her therapeutic journey. She would create a hero who would receive a 'Call to Adventure'. In classic fairytale terms, this could be to slay a dragon, rescue a damsel, escape from a tyrant, or find the solution to an impossible problem. Her hero would leave the security of home, loved ones and familiarity in order to venture into unknown territory. Every hero, no matter how brave, will be flawed in some small way. The whole purpose of the journey is for the hero to overcome insurmountable fears, to learn and by this to grow. This would provide the framework for her growth and exploration.

In choosing a hero, Emma would be focusing on the part of herself that was able to take action and to make changes. As her hero set out on the journey, and met with obstacles, Emma would have the opportunity to put into symbolic language the resistance that her ego put up to change.

Therapy

Emma very quickly engaged with archetypal material. In an early exploration, she connected strongly with three images: an eagle, a snake and a hag. She was drawn particularly to the eagle. As Emma began to create her hero's Journey, she chose to focus on the character of the eagle.

In the exploration, Emma took on the physical form of the eagle. Like an actor creating a role, Emma found out what it felt like to be the eagle, sometimes using pieces of costume to help her to 'get into' character. Once she had embodied the eagle, Emma spoke as the eagle, finding the eagle's particular way of talking and moving. I set up a structure in which I could interact with her as an objective third party, so I could focus on any aspect of the eagle that I felt warranted attention. At any point Emma could 'come out of character' if she was feeling uncomfortable or wished to reflect on her experience.

Right from the start, Emma had identified strongly with the eagle who was female. She moved with soaring movements and swooped around the room, enjoying the eagle's freedom and gracefulness. As the story developed, the eagle was drawn to a golden door and found herself in a garden which she was very attracted to. The eagle flew around the garden and then settled in the branches of a pomegranate tree, from which she was able to see other characters in the garden: a woman who was underneath the tree, a snake who was wound round one of the branches of the tree and a hag who was in another part of the garden. At this point Emma chose to leave the character of the eagle and embody the woman. She immediately became very tearful and expressed a need to be hugged by her boyfriend.

8. Joy

At the end of the session, Emma reflected on the experiences she had undergone. She was surprised at the emotions she had felt when she took the role of the woman and chose this character to represent her hero. She was also relieved that the hag had not frightened her and commented on the hag's capacity to see beauty in ugliness, and her ability to see through things to the reality beneath them. She made no mention about her feelings for the snake but it became apparent that she had ambiguous feelings about it.

It was clear from this session that the characters of the eagle, snake and hag were important metaphors for Emma since they had recurred several times in the session. She was attracted to the power and freedom of the eagle, and it seemed to represent an aspect of her inner self that she liked and aspired to. I was expecting Emma to choose the eagle as her hero since she had engaged with it so strongly, so it was a complete surprise to me when Emma switched allegiance from the eagle to the weeping woman under the tree. This is very significant in a drama therapy session, as the hero acts as the container for how the client sees herself. What Emma seemed to be saying, was that she knew she had the capacity to be powerful and to express her freedom but the woman was a more truthful representation of her current emotional state.

It was significant also that Emma had brought her boyfriend into the drama at the moment at which she had connected with the woman's emotions. When a client brings someone from their own life into the fictional world of the drama, it often means that either there is a boundary issue or that this is an area where they are holding a lot of emotion. It emerged later that Emma's relationship with her boyfriend was the key to the work we were to do together. In fact, she had not told her boyfriend about her decision to work with me, even though it was her habit to confide in him about everything. Emma had revealed through the drama her struggle between her dependency and the powerful forces within her. The weeping woman contrasted strongly with the characters of the eagle, snake and hag. Emma was showing me that she was a vulnerable young woman who needed her boyfriend to keep her safe.

Crisis

Emma's whole world was thrown into crisis when she started exploring her sexuality with another man. Emma's new partner offered her many of the things she had expressed in her sessions with me: joy, desire, sexuality, play, spontaneity. However, she found herself caught in a web of confusion in which she was afraid to leave the safe haven her current boyfriend offered and was afraid to meet the uncertainty with the new man. The fact that this coincided with confronting a monster in her hero's journey was significant.

At a certain point in every hero's journey, the hero is challenged to face a demon. In therapeutic terms, the demon represents a part of ourselves that we fear, hate or deny and often project into the outside world. If our demon is slain, it is likely that it will return in a different form as we integrate shadow elements of the self.

For Emma the demon was a monster. She created a large and very ugly mask in red and black pastels to express it. Monsters seem to provoke a very primordial response and often become projections for the rage that we have felt in childhood. Emma saw the monster as a meeting with her anger. As Emma explored the monster she released extremes of physical and vocal rage from behind the mask. Her monster was a wounded, trapped, blindly raging beast. There was an uncontained, unboundaried feeling in the way she expressed herself.

At the end of each session, she would resolve to leave her boyfriend, so that she could discover who she was without the prop that he represented. Yet the following session she would return more confused than ever.

Supervision

I took Emma's case to supervision because I had read Freddie Strasser's book *Existential Time-Limited Therapy*. I was unsettled and perplexed by the case, particularly by what had kept Emma so stuck and unable to act on her decisions. I hoped that the existential approach could shed light on Emma's reason for leaving the therapy and I was interested to see how existential perspective could deepen my understanding of my work with other clients.

Freddie first questioned me about my expectations for the therapy and explained that my first instinct had been to work on Emma's anger, facilitating Emma to find means to express, release and resolve anger using the hero's journey as a container for her emotions.

Freddie went on to ask what were Emma's expectations of the therapy and we deliberated on the fact that while Emma's presenting problem had been anger, she had focused more on her need for guidance and finding inner harmony within herself. I became aware that Emma's expectations were considerably higher than mine, which told me a lot about Emma.

Freddie introduced me to the way the existential approach would work with Emma. The therapist's role would be to reduce her expectations and to facilitate her in clarifying her world-view. He elaborated what he meant by world-view and reflected that I had an opportunity to use the metaphors of the drama to explore Emma's world-view. He demonstrated how this examination would reveal the ambiguities and contradictions within Emma's world-view and their impact on her thinking, feelings and behaviour. In challenging Emma's ambivalences, this would give Emma the impetus to continue working on herself after the therapy was completed.

We went on to discuss what her needs were originally and that they had shifted from her original intention to work on anger. What did this shift indicate? What did Emma mean when she said she wanted guidance, Freddie asked?

I recalled how Emma's need for guidance had been a recurring theme in our work together. I explored with Freddie the implications of Emma's need for the drama therapy to answer her questions, which was followed by her confusion when she was unable to act on the answers she had given herself. It seemed the subtext of what Emma was saying to me was that she believed that she was unable to make decisions for herself.

Freddie had drawn my attention to the fact that Emma had indicated some of the contradictions within her world-view in the first few minutes of our work together.

Joy: My World-View

Freddie was interested to know how Emma had expressed her emotions. I was called to remember the strong impression Emma had made on me when she was exploring the eagle. Through her fluid and graceful movements she had expressed joy. How Emma expressed this emotion through the drama would reveal certain facets of her world-view, Freddie told me, which would help to build up a picture of the values that had become rigidly sedimented in Emma and had led to her confusion and her decision to stop the drama therapy. Freddie asked me how I expressed joy. How did my expression of joy reveal facets of my world-view? If I could understand this then maybe I could also better understand Emma.

As I looked at my own experiences of joy, I remembered how much joy I had experienced when I was pursuing a career in the theatre. Performing had been extremely important to me in my mid-twenties when I was the same age as Emma. Indeed it had been close to an obsession. When I was expressing myself through performance, I felt fully and vitally alive. When I was not, the rest of my life seemed very dull by comparison.

I remembered particularly my experiences as an alternative cabaret performer, in which the audience had the right to 'boo off' any act that didn't please them. Therefore the excitement of performing was always mixed with intense feelings of dread. On the day I was due to perform, I woke up with an uncomfortable feeling in my stomach, knowing that this was no ordinary day, but a day in which I could be publicly shamed. As the day progressed, the sick feeling fluctuated, reaching its height in the half-hour before I was due to go on stage, necessitating many trips to the toilet. My mind was haunted by memories of an occasion when I was indeed 'booed off' by an extremely drunk and rowdy crowd.

However, the moment I was announced and made my entrance, I felt an immense surge of energy. The sick feelings and fears instantly disappeared. All I was aware of was the response coming back from the audience and the almost poetic communication that was happening between us. It often felt as if they were eating out of the palm of my hand. My pleasure was always at its most intense when the communication between us was most intimate. It was a very powerful moment for me to have two hundred people totally captivated by my mad and totally meaningless antics on stage. The essence of the joy for me lay in the mixture of the dread of making an utter fool of myself and the exhilaration of giving myself a hundred per cent to the performance. This made it a highly addictive activity. In my own therapy I had become aware that performing fulfilled a need to be seen and to receive the approbation of others. It had satisfied the part of myself that had the permission to escape from myself and become truly alive.

With Freddie, I reflected how the joy of performing was highlighting a need inside me to discover my own approval and to perceive my own perfection. But what I was doing was concentrating all my energy on seeking the approval of the audience, casting agents and other professionals to show them how good and perfect I was. What I got back from them, were occasional moments of joy and exhilaration to feed my addiction, but also numerous rejections which served to challenge even further my fragile self-esteem.

In this session, Freddie and I explored what rejection meant to me. I looked at all the other occasions when I had experienced rejection and how this revealed an important behaviour pattern, or what Freddie called a rigidly sedimented value system. I realised how I had performed for my father in order to make him happy and through that had experienced joy at his approval of me.

I was fascinated how exploring the emotion of joy had led to discovering these key facets of my world-view, and realised that the purpose of dismantling my own emotion was to enable me to resonate empathetically with Emma's world-view. I could not dismantle Emma's world-view with her since she had left therapy. However, I could use my own experiences, the metaphors of the drama and what I had observed Emma express in order to gain more understanding of Emma's world-view and thus begin to elicit the key facets that had kept Emma rigidly sedimented.

Like me in the past, Emma earned her living from performing. She had revealed that she had an idealised idea of herself through the joy she had expressed through the eagle. Expressing the eagle enabled her to connect with her power and omnipotence: this was her perfection. Emma too sought approval from others. She had been seeking it from me from our very first meeting. And she too was clearly addicted to performing. She had performed for me. Performing brought her alive.

Security and Insecurity

I had been aware in the contrasts of dread and exhilaration in my own experiences as a performer that the interplay between security and insecurity had fuelled my emotions. But how did Emma deal with the insecurity of her professional life? Like me she had carved out a secure base from herself. I remembered how I had deliberately sought a stable long-term relationship, and Emma, too, had chosen a stable partner who had kept her secure and dependent. Like my own relationship, Emma's had not supported her in growing emotionally and fulfilling herself sexually.

Freddie urged me to explore what the metaphors of the drama were revealing about Emma's world-view. I was immediately drawn to focus on the garden containing the eagle, snake and hag and the monster. We went on to discuss what these metaphors meant for Emma in what she had said about them and how she had used them in her drama.

The garden carried resonance of the theme of security and insecurity. Emma was clear that the garden represented a secure place for her. I recalled Emma's enthusiastic description of the home she shared with her boyfriend, which had a tree growing through the living room. The garden in the drama also had a tree growing in it. While the garden represented security, home, and being protected, there were also elements in the garden that Emma felt ambivalent about.

I was as aware as Emma was of the archetypal associations in these symbols. The snake in the tree carried associations of the tempter in the Garden of Eden and masculine sexuality, and I could not ignore the fact that Emma was soon to be tempted sexually by a new man, which would threaten every aspect of her secure world. In a later session, Emma elected that the snake should enter the woman in order to make her hero stronger. Emma was unsure about the hag. She commented on the hag's ability to see the reality beneath the surface, but she was also aware of her potential to do harm. Was the hag a wise woman or a witch? What was clear was that the snake and the hag represented potential threats to the security of the garden.

I was to remember at this point, my first impressions of Emma; her beautiful exterior masked by unflattering clothes and her approval-seeking behaviour. Was Emma saying through the hag and snake that in spite of her beautiful exterior, she knew there were things inside her that were potentially destructive?

Again my attention had been drawn to the uninhibited, ecstatic manner in which Emma had worked with the material. The sexual overtones were only too apparent. She wanted to consume and be consumed: to take the snake into her body as a classic image of masculine sexuality. Emma was seeking sexual fulfilment and she wanted to leave the secure world the garden represented.

If Emma was ambivalent about the snake and hag, Freddie pointed out, what did the monster mean to her? I was aware that the more rigidly sedimented aspects of Emma's world-view represented by the snake, hag and eagle were synthesised in the monster.

It was no surprise that Emma was ready to confront her monster, since she had left the garden and the false security that had kept her safe and dependent. She was now ready to meet with her anger and all the other things that had kept her trapped. She was liberated, but was she free?

What was also very clear in the way Emma had engaged with the monster, was that the monster was trapped. Through the monster Emma had discovered her rage, but this was not a rage that could be expressed and released. After its rage had been exhausted, the monster was left to face itself in its prison, as Emma was.

Through the supervision and Emma's subsequent actions, I saw Emma's fear of getting out of that prison and facing the world. Freddie explained that this would be showing up in all aspects of her life: her relationships, her family, and her work. This indeed was the case. Emma was locked into battle with her boyfriend, she complained that her looks were fading and she had no work. She turned up at sessions looking pale and unkempt, a shadow of her former self. She was in no state to go to auditions and engage in the competitive world of a dancer.

Freddie pointed out that this was where Emma's world-view and my world-view differed. I had been in prison, but I had got out of it. I was able to take risks. This put me in a position to help her, but it also left me feeling frustrated by the differences between her world-view and mine.

Confusion

Emma had expressed extremes of emotion through the monster. Freddie asked me what impact this had had on Emma's outside life.

I began to see that in the session Emma was courageous and able to take action, but outside of it she went back on all the decisions she had made. Thus Emma would return angry with herself for her inability to leave her boyfriend – this was her monster. She was guilty for the way in which she was torturing him by her indecisiveness and keeping him trapped, and she was angry with the new man for offering a freedom she felt unable to take. She presented catharsis after catharsis, which in most clients brings a resolution of issues, but for Emma it just kept her in the monster's den.

Emma and I had discussed how she was engaging with the monster within, and how something was stopping her from freeing herself from this beast. As I explored this avenue with Freddie, I recognised that gradually Emma's anger had been diverted away from the monster to being passively expressed towards me. There was an implication that I was in some way to blame for what had happened to her: that the drama therapy had added to her problems.

I had missed the opportunity to address the issue of Emma's anger towards me, and instead had been distracted by the problem of the monster. And yet the metaphor of the monster potentially had all the answers in it. Using the existential approach, if we delved deeply into the monster, we could get Emma to recognise the rigidly sedimented aspect of her world-view that was keeping her stuck. The monster facet would interconnect with all the other metaphors like the eagle, snake and hag. Each one would lead to her map of existence, her world-view.

Vacuum

We were now in our fourth session of supervision, and we were aware that with the absence of Emma to confirm our conclusions, we were having to rely on our own hunches for penetrating to the root of her problem. We knew that all our hypotheses needed to be suspended and put to the test experientially in the therapy. Unfortunately we could not do that with Emma. However, what we had established was that there were clear links between my world-view and Emma's.

The metaphors that Emma had worked with deeply fascinated me. Snakes, monsters and eagles were all symbols I have engaged with in my own self-exploration. Emma had also mirrored parts of myself in the way she moved and expressed herself. Bearing this in mind, Freddie asked me if I could role play Emma in such a way that I would entirely immerse myself in her personality.

As I role-played Emma, using the monster as a focal point, I felt myself being drawn down a very narrow tunnel. But as I proceeded down the tunnel, I became aware that it was not leading anywhere, and there was no point in going on. As Freddie questioned me as to what my experience was, I had a very strong sense of a vacuum in which, there were no answers, no choices, and where there was no possibility for action.

Emma's world-view linked with the 'black hole' I had discovered in Freddie's exploration of my joy of performing. Was there evidence of this in Emma's case? Certainly Emma was thrashing around in the black hole of her confusion. It was keeping her away from the joy she had expressed through the eagle, and she was a stuck in a vacuum in which she could not move forward. The vacuum was also her relationship with her boyfriend. She could not take a risk and burrow her way through the tunnel and find freedom for herself because this was too threatening to her rigidly sedimented behaviour patterns. Therefore she chose to withdraw and stay in the familiar territory of her relationship even though this was totally unsatisfactory for her. In doing this she was protecting her self-esteem. She was afraid of falling into the 'black hole' of low self-esteem which moving out of the relationship represented.

I had felt the same when I had a similar relationship crisis. I had known that the relationship was not right for me and yet I did not want to move into the 'black hole' that I knew I would face when I left the relationship. I would have to face myself, my insecurity, my dependency, and my aloneness in the world. In fact it took me many years before I was able to do this fully.

Emma could not at this time shake her value system to this extent. She had to stay in her familiar world. She was therefore stuck in the vacuum in which she was dependent on pleasing others and being accepted by them. She could not find additional meaning to her life in the form of fulfilling work and satisfying relationships but was trapped in the rigid values of her dependency and her need for security.

The role-play had demonstrated that we do not need to look at all the metaphors. We can choose any one and it will reveal the rigidly sedimented values in the client's world-view. The monster had revealed Emma's vacuum.

But how did this inter-connect with the other symbols in Emma's world-view – the eagle, the snake and the hag in the garden?

I knew that the theme of security had been prominent in Emma's relationship crisis. If the garden represented an uneasy but desirable security, then the eagle was in some ways above it. The eagle's security was when it was flying, and this was where Emma wanted to be. However, because she trapped in the monster's den, she could not find her wings. In order to move on she would have to wrestle with the reality of her earthly existence in which there was constant fluctuation between security and insecurity. Like me she would have to accept her imperfection and the limitations of the world.

Leaving

My initial contract with Emma for ten weeks had been extended in order to work through the relationship crisis. As financial pressures began to grow, I offered Emma a reduced rate so that she could resolve the issues she was working with. Towards the end of our work together, however, Emma's commitment was clearly wavering. She cancelled one session at short notice and for the last two sessions, she arrived between twenty minutes and half an hour late. She had been delayed both times by 'barneys' with the boyfriend she could not leave. In these sessions we were working to integrate aspects of her core self that had remained unresolved and progress was slow in the reduced time we had to accomplish this.

I was aware of Emma's growing emotional needs, and her inability to leave the relationship that was holding her back, and to take the action that she declared she wanted – to discover her own strength without the prop of either of the men who were claiming her. The vacuum was a truthful representation of Emma's rigid sedimentation of values, and it was a place she remained deeply committed to. Thus as we began to integrate the aspects of eagle, hag and snake that remained unresolved and to establish boundaries for her inner self, Emma began to take herself out of the therapy. Emma had made a clear statement. She was not yet ready to move out of the familiar world of the vacuum.

Working in the Future

The Hero's Journey is a structure that contains the chaos that the client is engaged with through the therapeutic journey. The journey is circular. The intention is for the hero to return to his homeland after meeting many challenges. With Emma the journey had stopped at a critical stage – the stage when she was starting to build a more secure base for her inner self. She had got though the most strenuous part of the journey but had stopped before her hero could receive a reward for her heroism. She had therefore denied herself the opportunity to acknowledge and reward herself for the battles fought with the monster, the pain endured and to recognise the new choices that were now available to her.

Emma was a case that came early in my work with private clients. My current practice is to take more time-establishing boundaries for the work, particularly with clients who, like Emma, are indicating that they may have boundary issues. The supervision drew attention to the confusion that Emma was presenting right from the start. I became aware how Emma's world-view coincided with mine, and of the differences that made us unique human beings. And yet by the end of our work together I became somebody that Emma blamed for bringing chaos and confusion into her life.

I now see that Emma's garden at the beginning was a rich resource, which if explored in greater depth, could have provided more information about her world-view. Freddie commented that he would not work in this way since existential therapy takes the approach that everything is of equal value and connects with everything else, so any starting point is valid. Drama therapy, however, works with journeys, and structures the therapeutic process through the beginning, middle, and end of a story. Therefore, the beginning stands as a clear place to cement the client's awareness of their world view before moving on to the more treacherous territory of the demon.

I had sought out the existential supervision because I wanted to know what had kept Emma so stuck and had led to her stopping the therapy. Was it financial pressures which I knew were growing at the time, or had I in some way failed her? I have reason to believe that Emma is still in the same situation as when she left the therapy and that she has not sought out another therapist. Emma expressed herself that she was overwhelmed by the powerful emotions she had encountered through the drama therapy, and that this combined with the relationship crisis had left her feeling particularly vulnerable. My feeling is that the drama therapy precipitated the relationship crisis which was already on the cards.

The therapy had become a bone of contention between Emma and her boyfriend and it can never be known if she stopped the therapy in order to placate him. There are many aspects of the case that I know now I would have handled better: I would have held her back from expressing her emotions until we had a securer therapeutic relationship; I would have explored our relationship more; and I would have challenged her more. Emma taught me many things and the supervision brought me understanding. Nevertheless, who knows what difference all these would have made to the final outcome – all I can say is that I hope they would have made a difference.

The existential point of view has been a rich contribution to the way I view my clients' journeys. I can begin to piece together their world-view and examine their sedimentations through the dramatic imagery they present. The supervision drew my attention to the 'thing itself' that was happening between Emma and me, and gave me insight about how I could make use of that awareness with other clients. Focusing on Emma's case has brought another frustration: the frustration that her hero's journey remains unresolved. The supervision brought awareness of the internal processes that hold my clients in their rigid value systems and me in mine. Indeed perhaps the most important aspect is that I am now clearer about my world-view and how it interacts with that of my clients.

The supervision has caused me to question from a new perspective my methods of working, while at the same time remaining aware of the differences between the two approaches. I am satisfied to find that the journeys my clients are currently engaged in is deepening in almost every respect. It is hardly surprising that many of them are bringing existential material to sessions, particularly around the area of their awareness of death. I continue to be inspired by the contribution that the existential approach can make to drama therapy, and I am now finding new ways that I can assist my clients in exploring their sedimentations using the language of drama.

9

Hate

Supervision is a vital element of the profession. Group or individual supervision with a professional therapist is important while training and while gaining experience. Peer or co-supervision is when two experienced professionals exchange views. Whether in training or whether practising as an experienced therapist, the purpose of supervision is to talk specifically about difficulties concerning particular clients and to discuss theoretical issues that might emerge. Both experienced and trainee therapists can easily overlook the most obvious issues in relation to the way they are working or ignore material brought by the client which could, when discussed, open up both the therapist's and the client's perspective. Therapists tend to work by themselves so supervision is a wonderful environment for discussing, analysing and opening up to alternative possibilities.

Supervision can be extremely exposing for the supervisee. The reason for this is that often a feeling of 'stuckness' with a client will have something to do with the supervisee's own issues. For instance, a common complaint is that 'The client is going nowhere – we keep going round and round in circles and we should have finished by now'. The issue may turn out to be more to do with the supervisee's own sense of how long a client should be in therapy and very little to do with the client. Once this awareness has been raised with the supervisee, their approach with the client may take on a different aspect. The client may now feel accepted and able to explore issues in a climate of trust. Sometimes the boundary between supervision and therapy is difficult to demarcate. The general rule is to aid the supervisee to realise their own issues and then it is their responsibility to explore their personal world-view.

In the case of co-counselling there is no supervisor-supervisee boundary and, therefore, the situation is even more delicate. In this process, the most important facet is to be open and accept criticisms even when they do not sound right. In order to do this, and to be effective, both parties need to surrender their own control and be able to reveal their own vulnerability. In the relationship between Alison and myself – father and daughter – this situation is compounded and is more delicate. For my part it has been difficult, especially at the beginning, to accept that if we wanted to be successful in this enterprise I had to share with Alison my most intimate weaknesses and shame. It was not easy, but when it worked, this was one of the most rewarding exercises for me.

Alison and I have worked together since she left her university course in London and we co-authored our previous book *Existential Time-Limited Therapy* through e-mail. Through this medium, telephone and occasional visits we have developed a skill by which we exchange our therapeutic experiences, rise above our differences, discuss our own issues and sustain an open relationship. We are frequently surprised how we both overlook the most obvious issues that might facilitate or hinder the therapy. As an example of this mutual effort, Alison narrates a co-supervised case study.

The Paradox of Hate

The First Session
Saskia marched into my therapy room and immediately took the single armchair, leaving me to sit on the two-seater sofa. She was in control. And that is how she wanted it to be – or rather that was how she was able to cope with coming to see a therapist, which she vowed she would never do because 'it was only for those sissies who run away with their emotions rather than using their rational brain'.

Questions, questions, questions. The first twenty minutes were devoted to Saskia asking me numerous, and personal, questions about my qualifications, my relationship status, my experience. Essentially, was I worthy of working with her? The more questions she asked, the more I wondered whether I was capable of enduring the onslaught. She finally slowed down by saying that she was disappointed that I was not older since she had a picture of a therapist as more mature. Indeed, she even added a few years to my actual age. How to make your therapist feel happy!

She finally justified her interrogation by saying that in life, she respected very few people and she needed to know whether I would be one of those people. I finally asked my first question 'Who were these other people'. Saskia replied that they were her mother, partner, and an older business friend. 'And what do they have in common?' I asked. This was more complicated, but in essence, they were all people who were able to take a broader stance on the world, not be limited by the trivia of life and to have the capacity for self-awareness. She hated stupid, lazy people and felt that people who did not maximise their potential were not worthy individuals.

Usually in the first session I leave plenty of room for clients to ask me questions. The reason being that afterwards, as therapy progresses, questions tend to be turned around so that the client has to think about their reason for asking. It also ties in with whether as a therapist one should or should not self-disclose. Generally, it is important for me to think carefully before revealing anything about me because of the possible ramifications. For instance, I once commiserated with a client about her migraines and disclosed how I felt that therapy had largely been my cure. A couple of weeks later, this client revealed that she had felt inadequate because of my revelation because she would never be able to do the same.

Saskia's flood of questions sent me into quite a headspin. I was not able to think fast enough about whether my answers were appropriate or whether there would be possible ramifications later in our therapeutic relationship. I therefore answered as honestly as possible, without expanding too much on the themes. However, I could feel myself shrinking into the couch and wondering when this battering would stop and how and when I could gain some control. As I asked myself that question, I could also hear my own therapist saying 'Alison, it's not that you want to control others, but you hate being controlled by them'. Well, here I was, in the thick of it.

Background

Saskia's father had been in the foreign service and her earliest memories were of the family in Asia. By the time, she was six, they had settled in Australia and her father had been discharged from the army. She had an elder brother and sister both of whom she was in contact with, although the brother, who trained as a doctor, chose to live an isolated existence in a remote area of Australia.

Her father moved from the army into business and the family became relatively affluent. The children were moved from a local school to a fee paying Catholic school. Saskia began to hate school. She felt she was singled out as not being good enough in terms of the 'right' background and felt that she was different from the other girls. She remembers her father as being unpredictable but highly stimulating. He was a stickler for correctness, but also able to flaunt society's conventions. He could be amusing and then lose his temper for no apparent reason.

The most significant event in Saskia's life was the divorce of her parents when she was fifteen. Her father walked out, leaving Saskia and her mother virtually penniless. He paid for her two siblings to finish their education, but refused to pay for Saskia, reasoning that she was not clever enough to go to university. From that moment Saskia became the parent, looking after her mother and also funding herself through university. Money became the object of her life, and still is the driving force for Saskia's existence.

Saskia is now thirty one and has worked on endless calculations to ensure that millions can be earned before her retirement, which she aims to achieve in ten years. She works as a consultant in the computer business as well as having investments. She works herself into absolute exhaustion and then collapses for several months before her drive for money rekindles itself.

Co-Supervision

I believe that much of the work that happens in the therapeutic relationship depends not only on the client doing the work, but also the therapist in terms of processing their own emotional material. Part of this reflective work is achieved in supervision and what is interesting about this particular case study is that my father acted as my supervisor. A father-daughter relationship also elicits issues pertinent to control, so what emerged were not only my own reflections as germane to my client, but also my own feelings in relation to my father.

I have often reflected that when I feel stuck with a client, it turns out to be partly my own issues that have been jolted. Saskia was certainly a case in point. Control, or rather being controlled, is a personal theme that is persistent in my life. So, what is evoked in me when I feel that someone is controlling me? My behaviour is usually to defend myself, to try to take some control back. Why do I do it? The answer lies around anxiety, that if I don't defend myself or make myself known in some way I will end up as a nothing, a nobody, being trampled underfoot by the world.

In supervision we discussed this further because unless I amplified my own issues of being controlled, my work with Saskia would end up as a battleground as we both vied for dominance and there would be little or no empathy in our relationship. Already I was questioning whether I could work with someone whose values were so alien to my own, who appeared to have little or no empathic faculty within herself.

To be in control, to succeed, to be liked were somehow all linked. These materialised when my father asked, 'What do you have to do not to be rejected?' The answer lay around my sometimes over-defensive attitude, my tendency to blame situations or people, rather than take responsibility for my own inadequacies.

These fears are also apparent in my relationship with my father and in supervision with him. He has more experience than I do both in life and in his years as a therapist. He helped me enormously during my training, but at that point he was still my father, my educator, and the person who knew more than me. As I have gained my own experience, I have also had to question these former assumptions and to grow into a daughter as an individual and a therapist with her own knowledge and expertise. The question I often still ask myself is 'Where is the line between defending myself against knowing that I might not be right and having a valid argument for the way that I have been working?'

A similar pattern arose when we discussed my own feelings behind my words 'enduring the onslaught'. What was the threat to me when she questioned me? My answer lay in the direction of my own fear of 'exposing' myself as an inadequate therapist. In addition, of course Saskia had made it quite clear that she wanted a more than adequate therapist, which fed directly into my own self-esteem. 'What would happen if you did fail, that you weren't good for her', my father asked. This was getting close because in the past I have experienced or chosen situations where I have not succeeded in the way that I had hoped and I do not like the experience of failing. Re-experiencing these emotions of failure and my own determination not to fail allowed me to reflect on the kind of questions I might be able to ask Saskia when the situation arose again.

On a more theoretical level, my fear about being controlled links in with the discussion in Chapter Two about unreflective and reflective emotions. At an elementary level, when Saskia began her 'onslaught' I was reacting in an unreflective manner. My reaction was to defend myself, to prove that I was good, to show Saskia that I was not one of those people she despised. Yet as soon as I became aware of what I was doing, or rather my emotions became reflective, I began to see a whole array of possibilities. I could carry on defending myself or I could begin the process of therapy and try to understand both for myself and Saskia what was actually happening. The hard truth, though, is that guilt also accompanies the awareness. In my case, it was guilt around the fact that I had wanted to control and to prove myself.

What is my world-view when I do not need to do this? An immediate response is fear. Who am I? How do I conduct myself? Will everyone trample over me? Surely, it is easier to be the person I was, rather than face changing my self-construct? The answer lies somewhere in between, with the ability to accept that I do not like being controlled but that I do have alternative responses when the situation occurs.

Discussing with my father the pitfalls of therapy and my issue of being controlled, we talked about how it is so common for therapists (even those from a phenomenological orientation) to fall into the trap of wanting to 'do' or to 'achieve' something. Experience also dictates that the moment this happens, the therapeutic alliance is upset as the client also feels that they must 'do' something. The greatest gift for both oneself and the client is the ability to 'be', to not have expectations, to embrace the unknown and to allow the process to unfold. Therapy is about being empathic and allowing the client to reveal their world-view and for the therapist to challenge and explore their ambiguities. If I could adopt the stance of not expecting from myself, then the chances are that I would not fear the 'onslaught', allow the process to unfold at its own pace and to find empathy and understanding with my client.

This rumination led to the proposition that there was a good chance Saskia also threatened other people and that this aspect could also be examined. Nevertheless, the main focus of our co-supervision centred on how Saskia had begun to impart her world-view in just one session. She hated stupid, lazy people, which in itself was saying that lazy was bad and hard working was good. In this one statement, both a sedimentation and a value had been revealed, which was important for me to explore in our sessions because the chances were that issues around 'laziness' and 'badness' would connect with Saskia at some level.

Other questions that also emerged in our supervision were: why did Saskia need to adopt this style of behaviour? What was she defending herself against? What emotions lay behind this stance? In her revelations about 'stupid, lazy people who did not maximise their potential', Saskia was also indicating her own values, so what was so important about being clever, energetic and able to achieve?

A common mistake of any supervisee is to try to find answers or to force the reflections raised in supervision onto the client in the next session. Supervision is about raising one's own awareness. However, the specifics discussed with the supervisor must be 'bracketed' because the client has also had time in-between to reflect and to grow. Posing a question or making an interpretation which reflected a previous session maybe totally out of context to the person now sitting in front of you.

Anger

Indeed, it did not take long to emerge. Saskia had finally decided to seek help because of her anger. No, she did not really mind her anger but it affected other people and especially people who were important to her. When both her partner and her sister suggested that she seek help, she began to feel that maybe something was not quite right.

We spent a good deal of the next session exploring Saskia's anger. It was an amazing journey as she described the mastery and power she felt when she was angry. As she spoke, her body physically rose as she took command of her space. She felt good, she was exhilarated and most important of all, she was safe and in control. From her position of anger, she was able to annihilate anything or anybody, as she so desired. I felt her passion and a profound sense of sadness, which were both aspects that I bracketed hopefully to explore at a later date.

Saskia was not showing any anger as she recounted the experience, but instead she was able to picture herself in her temper. She was describing her anger as if she was there and I was able to imagine also, from my own perspective, her sense of anger. Any questions I asked did not move her out of the feeling state but only helped Saskia go further into the power she felt.

We had agreed to work together for fourteen weeks, since this conveniently led us up to Christmas. The follow-up sessions would be after a break in March. After that we agreed on a further twelve weeks, which also conveniently took Saskia to another long holiday she had planned.

Co-supervision

In our co-supervision session, we discussed Saskia's anger and how it was an intrinsic aspect of her world-view, since it helped her in her task of maintaining superiority and control and denying her feelings of low self-esteem. Again, it was closely linked to Saskia's fear of rejection, loneliness, of not being right and the feelings associated with these. Indeed, anger was a strategy designed to prevent any of these emotions touching her because her fear of abandonment or rejection was so intense.

Saskia was living in a state of unreflective anger. She knew she got angry but her cognitive and emotional awareness of what it was or why she got angry was virtually non-existent. In a state of anger she could prove to herself that she was in control, that she was superior to everyone else. To become aware of her underlying lack of self-esteem and the accompanying emotions would involve Saskia in an enormous struggle. She might try to eliminate both her anger and guilt at the same, time which is an impossibility since both are existential givens and both were intrinsically linked to her self-construct.

Anger is a complex emotion and one that is often used in the therapeutic situation. Either a client is very explicit with their anger, as with Saskia, or they are unable to express it at all. Self-help books write about the importance of anger release, but I believe that although this may sometimes be beneficial, the anger itself (or the lack of it) and what it means must be explored and clarified. It appeared that in the case of Saskia, anger was partly a defence against experiencing her underlying emotions.

After co-supervision, I felt it was important to go deeper into Saskia's anger so that the unreflective emotions could become reflective. Saskia's world-view was unravelling itself and part of my task was to explore this more and to begin challenging the ambiguities that revealed themselves both in her behaviour patterns and in her emotional and cognitive spheres.

Paradox

As therapy proceeded I realised that Saskia's life was one of polar extremes, or what are known as paradoxes. For instance, she hated people who she felt were lazy, who did not better themselves in some way, who lived off the state, and who lived life in an unquestioning manner. And although on the surface Saskia lived her life at a frenetic pace, it emerged that at various periods in her life she had spent months doing nothing except watch television, drink copious amounts of alcohol, eat the foods she normally disdained and generally laze around. The irony was that these were the times when emotionally she felt most at peace with herself, when she expected nothing of herself and did not think too much about money. Indeed, she did not think much about anything. This ideal of peace was also her major aim. She felt that if she could sort out her finances, she would be able to find peace. Work itself was hectic, and ruled her life, whereas peace would give her day-to-day control over her life. The question I asked myself and eventually Saskia was whether she could achieve this peace she so yearned for, when at the same time she despised what it stood for.

Another paradox was her thoughts about people who lived through their emotions. Saskia felt they were stuck, that they were self-obsessed and that these were the kind of people who were unable to move forward and take possession of their life. At the same time, she felt enormous respect for her partner, who had taken the trouble to see a counsellor and to work through his emotional traumas. Saskia, too, was bemused by herself. She could not understand why she would cry when she came to see me, why she felt emotionally drained after a session and why she would spend the days in between therapy reliving moments in her life that she had felt unimportant.

Tears would well up when she spoke of her feelings of abandonment after her father had 'dismissed her as worthless'. Yet she, too, had walked out on situations and people and left them to fend for themselves. Saskia was riddled with guilt about leaving her mother in another city with very little money, yet she justified not giving her an allowance by saying that her mother should have her dignity and instead would spend money on lavish holidays that she would take with her mother and partner.

Saskia felt sorry for herself and also felt intense anger when she thought about her father. She wanted to control her feelings because she felt out of control when they emerged. She felt love and respect for her father and she also hated him. Control became part of Saskia's work view.

Co-supervision

In one of our co-supervision discussions we came back to the issue of control and how the paradox was so apparent. Although control was an important manifestation of Saskia's world-view, it was becoming apparent that it was far more complex. As Saskia began to reveal her emotions, such as her anger and hate towards her father and her intense dislike of school, she also disclosed her values. It was imperative that she proved to the world and her father that she was clever, almost to prove that her father was wrong and should never have abandoned the family. She had to excel more than others to prove that she was not rejected or inferior to others as she had experienced at school and with her father. Therefore, in order to be a somebody (rather than a nobody), her life strategy had been to prove to herself and others that she was clever, that she could make money and lots of it. It was almost as if the more money Saskia made, the cleverer she was, the more respected and likeable a person she had become.

Interwoven with these issues was her wish to have peace and peace for Saskia was lying around and being the person she so much despised in other people. Of course, the moment she realised she was this person, she felt enormous waves of guilt, which drove her back to her frenetic life at work. This kind of guilt was unreflective and therefore impossible to eliminate. If she forfeited her feelings of guilt, then she would have to grapple with the neurotic guilt that would replace it. At the other extreme, when Saskia was working at her frenetic pace, she had to ensure that she was always on top, otherwise she had to face her feelings of insecurity. The paradox being that whether she was in her 'peaceful' state of doing nothing, or living life to the full, she was still having to face the guilt and anxieties that arose from these insecurities.

Self-Construct – Control

Saskia put an extraordinary amount of energy into remaining in control of her life. This was highlighted when we began the second module of twelve weeks, when in the intervening three months she and her siblings had persuaded their mother after more than fifteen years to sue their father as part of the divorce settlement. Their father tried to contact each of the siblings in turn. Saskia was the only one who decided to talk to him on the telephone and she relished it. Her excitement was intense as she related the conversation to me. She felt that 'despite all he had put her through she could finally ram her success down his throat'. She was equal if not better than him in terms of the amount of money she had made, the relationships she had formed and her general awareness about the world. It felt to me as if the lawsuit was Saskia's revenge against her father for trying to ruin not only her life but also her mother's. I asked her how she had felt during the conversation and she replied 'For a moment I felt sorry for him, but then I remembered everything that he had done, and all I felt was overwhelming pleasure'.

It is often revealing to explore the opposite values iterated by a client, so a series of questions I asked Saskia were related to love and what it was like for her to love someone. Saskia loved her partner, her mother and her siblings. She also admitted to having loved her father before he walked out. She felt accepted by these close relationships even when she lost her temper or did not accept what they had to say. 'What is it like when you are angry with them?' I asked. 'Wonderful at the time, but I feel awful afterwards' she replied. 'I feel so guilty that I've upset them when they've done so much for me'. On further probing, Saskia elaborated and then began to realise that trust in someone is the ability to love and hate at the same time and to still be accepted and to accept the other.

There still remained in the back of my mind the question raised in co-supervision about what it was like for Saskia when she was unable to control situations and hence her feelings. We knew that she had plenty of strategies for gaining or regaining her control, but what did she experience when she felt out of control?

The answer or at least part of the answer emerged when she discussed her anxieties about having dinner with an old school friend of hers who had flown in from Los Angeles. Although she had not seen this friend for about ten years, she had followed her progress over the years and she knew that this woman had gone from strength to strength in her chosen career and looked like 'a million dollars'. They had been friends at school because they were both seen as different by the prevailing peer group. Saskia had been labelled as 'lower class' and her friend as the school tart and hence both were ostracised. This was the first time I had seen Saskia anxious. She was unsure of herself and how to prove to this woman that she was also successful. As we probed deeper into the anxiety, Saskia was able to reveal that when she felt rejected she also felt intense loneliness; that there was no-one who could understand who she was and how she felt. Proving to others that she was right was not only a strategy to enable herself to be heard but also a way for Saskia to show others how good she was.

The pending dinner date turned out to be more complex, for Saskia was also wrestling with some of the issues that we had talked about in our sessions. How much of the 'new' Saskia should she reveal? How could she talk about the variations of 'success', which included external worldly goods, but also her inner sense of finding a peace that might not include financial gain? She felt that if she spoke about this her friend was even more likely to reject her, since she imagined that any friendship would be based around monetary acquisitions.

The irony was that the following week, after Saskia had met her friend, she related that none of these fears had materialised because she had realised that this person represented all her old values and Saskia had made the decision not to reveal anything about herself or to continue any friendship.

This incident also exposed the significance of other people's opinions and how these dovetailed with Saskia's need to control. Another aspect of this related to her own sense of possible failure. About a year before seeing me, Saskia had designed and built a 'dream house' in a wealthy part of the city. She was in her element. She got so much pleasure in watching and overseeing the building work and yet once it was complete, she decided not to move in. The house represented her fantasies and yet she was afraid of showing the world what these were in case they rejected them and hence her.

Co-Supervision

Control was a theme that kept emerging in our supervision sessions. We talked about how it was a strategy for survival to prevent the feelings of inadequacy and self-esteem issues from emerging. In order to become a somebody, Saskia had to develop pride and this she could literally monitor by the amount of assets she could count. However, it was not enough to know that she had money in her bank account, she also needed to let others be aware of her success. She could not face losing control because then she was a nobody. Not only could she not allow herself to contemplate this, she could not allow others, including those close to her, to see this inferior side of her. She had to keep her sense of pride and dignity at all costs.

From an existential point of view, in order to maintain this self-construct, Saskia was fighting against one of the important givens. She would not allow herself to face any form of anxiety, be it related to insecurity, inferiority, loneliness, or disapproval. Thus her desire to keep constant command turned into a neurotic aspiration which finally led her to questioning her motives and examining her issues around self-esteem.

The Therapeutic process

I often wonder what it is that therapists do in therapy except to 'be there' for the client in many senses of the word. At present I believe that my job is to allow the client to become aware of new possibilities. This is a twofold process where at one level I ask questions that open the client's awareness, to allow him/her to think beyond their original point of view. For instance, at times I could not believe how rigid and single-minded Saskia's opinions about people were. At the moment of bracketing this reflection, I would also think of a question that would allow her to think about her opinions without adding my own value judgement and then use Saskia's own words as much as possible. This might emerge as 'How do you think your friend felt when you got angry with her for expressing her viewpoint?' I used this a lot with Saskia since it had the effect of making her pause and after a few weeks she began to talk about other people's feelings and how these affected her.

The other part of the process is to home in and ask questions that dig deeper in one particular aspect, which allows the client to access both their cognitive and emotional facets at a profound level. Although, initially, Saskia did not see the point of looking into her past when we explored the time when her father left the family, she reached inside herself and became aware of an overwhelming sadness. In another session, she described in detail the sense of peace she felt when she allowed herself to stop and indulge in the forbidden fruits, or rather the aspects of life that she forbade because they smacked of the laziness she so despised in others.

Saskia would ponder during the week on the issues that were raised. Sometimes she would elaborate and come to realisations about something that had been discussed the previous week. At other times she wanted more from me, not really believing that she trusted someone who she did not really know. As she began to trust the process more, she began to bring in more memories of her past and to make her own links as to why she so desperately needed to be in control.

Relationships

During the first module of fourteen weeks, I found the beginning of each session was like a battleground, as Saskia needed to justify and rationalise coming to see me. I realised that I felt a need to defend myself. I worked more cognitively than I normally do, almost to the point of entering into a debate. I remember hearing myself point out one of her many paradoxes and then wondering what it was that I needed to defend against and how others in her life might also be reacting to her.

I had to be so careful to suspend or bracket my own thoughts and to allow Saskia to explore her own meanings, to find her own connections and possibilities of where she wanted to go. Although I found our relationship difficult, once I had suspended my own judgements and begun to understand and empathise with Saskia's world-view, I also learnt more about my own control/judgement issues. In my eyes Saskia became more human, she showed human frailties and also an enormous strength.

New Possibilities

The incident with Saskia's old school friend occurred close to the end of our second module. A different atmosphere surrounded our final sessions. Saskia was ready to move on and to embrace what she had discovered into her lifestyle. She had planned a long vacation and was thinking about stopping the consultancy work she was doing for other people and spending more time working for herself. Her desire was to spend more time with her close friends, get healthy and lose weight.

Saskia had certainly opened herself up to new possibilities, yet I had had a strong sense that she still over-emphasised the need to be in control. She certainly appeared more humble and able to embrace other people's perspective. She had explored how people she knew and loved were successful in other dimensions apart from monetary gain. She was more aware of her emotions around hating, loving, and more open to her sadness, loneliness and anxieties around rejection. Control and her issues around her anger were part of her life, yet her definition and understanding of her sedimentation was now broader and gave her the space for reflection. She understood what control meant in terms of her behavioural strategies, emotional defences and also how the whole stratagem had helped her achieve success. Money would be able to give her the time for peace, but she could not relinquish her idea that other people only measure her in the amount of dollars she owned.

Summarising, Saskia was able to open up and examine her worldview and to challenge her sedimentations and ambiguities around control/not being in control, approval/rejection, love/hate, peace/frenetic work. She was able to understand the effect of her father leaving the family and the strategies she employed to deny the underlying emotions of sadness and pain. One of the most important changes was from being adamant that she was right to the realisation that other people had valid points of view, even if different from hers. Paradoxically she had begun to live within the paradoxes.

Reflections

In the same way that I do not believe in telling clients what to do, I also believe that the same adage applies to supervision – the exception being when ethical codes of practice are breached. I have had to learn both as a supervisee and supervisor not to feel I am being controlled by suggestions from a supervisor or to be controlling with my supervisees. My own defences as a supervisee are sometimes apparent in my supervisees when they may not reveal an aspect of the way they are working for fear of my reaction.

Fear of rejection, failure, abandonment and the strategy of controlling and being controlled have all been key issues in the above case study. The complex interrelationship between myself and Saskia, myself and my father, Saskia and her world, myself and my supervisees all had an impact on each other. It is impossible to sort out what it is that actually has the impact in the therapeutic situation except to say that the therapist's personal awareness leads to an opening up of one's world-view, which then allows the therapeutic relationship to expand in new directions. Therapy without supervision is like eating with no food and although confronting and sometimes painful, I believe it is vital to the whole process. Working with my father as an equal (which also means that he has to reveal his own weaknesses and sedimentations) has been and continues to be something very special.

10

Epilogue

At the beginning of the therapy, Jacob presented himself as a mentally retarded person. He spoke of his brain damage at birth or during his infant years. He was told that he was kept in a hospital for a long time and classified as a mentally handicapped child well before his school age.

Jacob was forty six years old when he first came to see me. Whenever I think of him, I always visualise him as that tall, good looking person with a small beard, who could not only experience things very deeply, but could also narrate them without much effort. On top of all this, Jacob had a good sense of humour and was able to laugh at himself. Many times in the sessions, we found ourselves laughing for a considerable time. It was remarkable to me that this person labelled 'mentally retarded' had the capacity to describe things with such clarity. He was able to go right to the essence of situations, devoid of any preconceived ideas. Indeed, whenever I think of the phenomenological approach, Jacob always comes to my mind.

Jacob puzzled me: he had been labelled, treated, and accepted himself as a mentally 'disabled' person. Yet he spoke, looked and behaved like a person of the highest intellect. In fact, I only noticed his 'disability' when he signed his cheque. He did it very slowly, letter by letter and digit by digit. Yet, in spite of this, I spontaneously registered him in my mind as 'The Professor', an image I maintained permanently.

I have worked with Jacob for the last seven and a half years. Sometimes I feel that such a co-dependence has developed between us that our therapy will never end. We began with one session weekly, than we gradually reduced this to fortnightly and finally to one session per month. He comes to me for therapy and I get from him an uncontaminated philosophy of life.

We began our therapy course as the result of an accident at his workplace. Jacob was referred to an institute for counselling and then referred to me by a female counsellor, as she felt I would be a more suitable person to deal with Jacob's 'problems'. However, the accident was barely mentioned during the course of the therapy as it was overshadowed by events that had started many years earlier. Jacob knew about therapy; in his youth, he was sent to various specialist institutions, amongst others to a child psychology institute. Finally, he received his 'green card'. Later in life, he had been treated with electrical shock therapy in a hospital. The green 'disability card' accompanies him to this day and he is now employed as a helper, sorting letters and photocopying.

In his first session, Jacob vented huge, accumulated anger against two female superiors who had been in charge of him many years before, in two jobs, for 15 years. The issue of his anger is still prevalent in therapy, albeit to a lesser degree.

Therapy

We agreed on an open-ended module of therapy on a weekly basis. He paid the subsidised fee to the referring institute. The main issues in the therapy revolved around his anger at his ex-employers, going back twenty five years, his sexuality, resentment of a black colleague, bullying at school, and meaninglessness of his life. Early in the therapy, he recounted his story. He was told, as soon as he was able to comprehend it that he was a brain-damaged child and that he would have to accept the fact that he was disabled. In his words, he was lucky to have been born to a very warm, intellectual and closely bonded family, who functioned with as much harmony as was feasible. From his account, it appeared that the family was not only talented, but also caring and self-reflecting and that they treated Jacob with special care and love.

His mother, a teacher of children with learning disabilities, made every effort to help Jacob develop his full potential. From the age of four until fifteen he was sent to a special school. When he was sixteen he started work and was employed in a variety of jobs. He had been a helper in a wine shop, an assistant in a hospital, had worked in an animal research department and finally, at the age of twenty one, he acquired a post with a charity organisation where he still works to this day.

My own opinion throughout these early stages of the therapy was that the disabled label that he was carrying throughout his life adversely affected Jacob's happiness. I knew that he was talented in music and sports and I felt that in all his activities this label must have made him an under-achiever. I was convinced that his world-view and his self-esteem must have been affected by these 'frustrations'. I was glad that I was able to suspend this preconceived idea and that I was able to follow Jacob's line of thought, which proved that my hypothesis was mistaken.

The Joy of Sexuality

At the age of fourteen, Jacob became attracted to a fellow student. In one of the sessions, he related an incident, which left a deep impression on him, and throughout the therapy we used this as a metaphor. Pia was an attractive young girl he met in class and they became good friends. One day she fell ill and Jacob frequently visited her in her room. The doctor thought her illness might lead to something serious such as pneumonia. She had a high temperature and an unpleasant cough.

Jacob began to describe a specific happening during her illness. As he entered her room, sorrow and compassion overpowered him when he saw her in that helpless and pitiful state. She was still coughing, and also belching. A fantasy overwhelmed Jacob in which he perceived her as totally dependent on him, to the extent that he was her doctor, 'saviour' and master of all 'that was inside her'. He not only felt in control, but also was moved by a very potent sexual arousal.

This fantasy accompanied him right through his life. All his sexuality depended on this image. While I was listening to his story, I was very careful not to prompt him prematurely. Had I done so, I believed that I could probably have impaired the development of an all-important, trusting relationship. I already knew that he had encountered problems with his previous therapist and that he had felt he could not reveal his sexually related thoughts to his therapist. I was focusing on his body language and was carefully listening to all the details of his story.

I had seen him for over seven and a half years, yet again and again at each session I was astonished how he got straight to 'the things themselves' in his naïve, yet at the same time sophisticated way. I was prompting and reflecting back. I was almost dazzled by the ease with which he became totally 'open' and by the ease and apparent lack of effort, it had taken him to 'tell all'.

He explained that apart from some doctors and a few women friends, only I knew his story. 'How is this? Could you expand on this?' I asked. He recounted that apart from his masturbation, which was based on his fantasy of Pia's belching; he had experienced no physical contact with women until he was twenty two years old. Then he had met an older woman who seemed ready to have sex with him. When she discovered and learned about his sexual fantasies, she rejected any sexual relationship with Jacob and suggested that he should seek professional help. I had expected that such a slight would have had a very damaging effect on his self-esteem and I waited to hear of his pain and other similar emotions. Nothing of the sort had happened. Jacob carried on happily with his fantasy combined with masturbation, until one day he went to his GP who asked him about his sex life.

According to Jacob, the doctor was very interested in psychology. As a result of Jacob's 'story', he advised him to see a psychologist. Jacob had no doubt in his mind that if he was referred to a consultant psychiatrist then he had no option but to go and see one. Thus, Jacob found himself in a psychiatric clinic, where his story intrigued the consultant and was of great interest to the clinic as a whole.

Other psychiatrists were called in and became involved in Jacob's case. As part of his treatment, he was taken to a room where he was shown video footage of a woman belching and each time she belched, he received a controlled electric shock (ECT). In other words, he was subjected to aversion therapy. The treatment lasted for a few months. I asked Jacob what the outcome was when treatment was completed. He had a cynical smile on his face and in a laughing tone said: 'These people thought they could deprive me of one of the greatest joys in my life; but they were wrong.' When Jacob found something humorous, he used to laugh heartily for a considerable time and I joined in the amusement.

The doctors evidently had the preconception that Jacob's fantasy was negative and an immense problem for him. I was intrigued for a long time how Jacob resisted their pressure. On rare occasions he visited prostitutes and asked them to co-operate with him in his 'ways'. Some of them were intrigued by these special sexual fantasies. To his amazement, some of them accepted him as he was. But most of them found his sexual habits peculiar, even though they co-operated.

We explored his sexuality from all angles. He made a great effort to survey all sexual perversions and after a while he found a similar fantasy in one of the magazines. In a way, he was pleased with this discovery because he could share it with somebody, but he was also upset about it as the uniqueness of his experience had vanished. He said: 'I do not know what to make of it. In a way, I feel special because of my unique fantasy. I do, however, wonder if there is anything wrong with me or not'.

He questioned whether those sexual aberrations like brutal sadism or different fetishes were better, worse or in the same category as his belching fetish. In his own way, he came to the conclusion that it was a matter of personal attitude; for him it was alright, as he did not inflict harm on anybody and it provided him with pleasure and joy. I was truly amazed how a person who was considered all his life to be mentally retarded came to this very profound conclusion on his own.

I was trying very hard to discover how Jacob could maintain his self-esteem in the face of all these rejections. The rejection of the women, who advised him to seek help, the opinion of the doctor who treated him for 'sexual aberration', none of them had affected his self-esteem. I laboured hard to with the need to suspend my own assumptions. In the back of my mind, I was convinced that Jacob's need to improve his life was thwarted by having a disability card which provided him with a comfort zone. The card implied to him that a disabled person could not achieve much because of his or her disability. It explained why Jacob gave up trying to create meaningful sexual and other relationships. Yet, this assumption proved flawed, as Jacob's musical achievements and his other explorations demonstrate.

Music

Coming from a musical family, Jacob realised at an early age that he was not only endowed with musical talent but was also deeply touched by music. He sang in a choir and plays the piano. He has an upright piano and plays for his own enjoyment.

During the early stages of the therapy, I urged him to challenge himself and explore how it was that he did not aspire to improve his musical talent. He found this exercise quite amusing. He smiled sheepishly and asked 'What for?' Why should he exert himself when he was happy with his piano playing as it was? Why should he put effort into other ambitious activities when in general he was able to accept himself as he was.

Now, I understood him. It was not the disabled label that made him less ambitious, but the fact that Jacob could not find any meaning in having aspirations to play the piano better or to improve his sexual relationships. He had totally accepted himself as he was.

Abuse at School

Jacob was thirteen years of age when he encountered the first threat to his physical being. He felt that he was well established in a special boarding school when two of his form mates started to bully him, threatening him in various ways. Jacob described this period as being filled with daily trepidation, awaiting unknown punishment. The culmination of this fear was the actual act of these two bullies. He was locked up in a dark cupboard and was left there for hours. Even his release, some hours later, could not assuage his awful shock, dread, fear, and helplessness.

Eventually one of the culprits was expelled from the school and the other consequently became less abusive. However, in therapy, this fear of helplessness, his loss of control, self-esteem, and isolation, all remained. Different, but equally threatening, events reinforced Jacob's anger and fear of falling into this dreadful lonely place.

Abuse at Work

As mentioned before, Jacob's presenting problem centred on the anger that he felt against two of his former female superiors. For seven years, he was subjected to the most provocative and humiliating abuse. It was as if one of these superiors unburdened herself of her troubles at Jacob's expense, transferring all her frustrations onto him. Jacob has already experienced difficulties in his previous job and was therefore determined 'to sit this one out'. This 'hell' lasted seven years.

Each morning he dreaded going to work, anticipating the outbursts of his superior. These sadly, but inevitably, followed. Jacob said there was no doubt that he was used as a scapegoat for all of his boss's disappointments and failures. His colleagues in the office who witnessed Jacob's constant humiliations never interfered, although they sometimes expressed their sympathy,. His influential father, who could have helped him, advised him to persevere with the job and suggested that the situation would resolve itself.

Indeed, the situation had changed somewhat. He was transferred to another department doing a similar job. His new boss was a smallish woman with a vile temper, and for a further ten years he was subjected to more abuse. In therapy, I prompted him to recount specific experiences, which he recalled by showing great anger. Yet again, his colleagues witnessed the abuse, sometimes with compassion and at other times with bored equanimity, but they offered no help. He complained to his director, but this simply made the situation worse. Jacob explored his anger incessantly in therapy and had become aware of many facets of this emotion. He spoke of his vindictive will to take revenge on the two women, the sadness of his predicament and of his frustration. Later in the therapy, he began to realise that his own anger and other associated emotions revealed his own vulnerability. It revealed his fear of being humiliated and isolated with loss of self-esteem. The anger enabled him to overcome his feelings of inferiority and made him somehow feel superior.

I asked him to describe similar experiences. It was not difficult for Jacob to relate the anger, the frustration, and loss of self-esteem to other memories and to one of the incidents of his long incarceration in the cupboard. As the memory of his anger subsided, he began to analyse his boss's possible motive for constantly humiliating him. He perceived her animosity as a protection of her own vulnerability. As she was not English, she felt somewhat out of place in a foreign environment. Jacob, on the other hand, was a large person, well at home in England, especially as he had a very influential father, so he argued.

Jacob concluded, that his boss, in order to protect her self-esteem and to guard her inferiority, invoked anger and other similar emotions. These then served her to feel superior and protected her self-esteem. Jacob's anger did not entirely vanish, but rather subsided and changed. This manifested itself in mighty laughter, when he visualised the grotesque situation they were in.

Fear of Losing his Job

Following these seventeen years of abuse, Jacob moved within the same organisation and became an assistant in the administration department. There was no more abuse and he enjoyed good human relationships. He had a good position and managed to obtain a nice one-bedroom flat. Yet the anger persisted and by chance he had ended up in my consulting room, as explained previously.

In his current environment, life had become a routine: going to work, returning home, playing music, and browsing through magazines with erotic pictures. In addition to this routine, Jacob had started visiting me first weekly, then fortnightly and finally monthly. Thus, his life was very regular, and included weekly visits to his mother. In therapy, however, as his anger towards his previous employers receded, so a new and powerful anger and fear appeared, this time against a black stranger. It appeared that his anger against this person was as persistent and rigid as his previous hatred of his supervisors. The important difference was, however, that it was accompanied by a deep-seated guilt. He knew there was something more unpleasant in harbouring those emotions. Innumerable times he repeated how he despised himself for hating somebody of a different race, because as a Jew he should have known better.

What emerged in the following sessions was Jacob's exploration of the meaning of his anger and guilt. He soon became aware that his emotions were there to protect his self-esteem. That is to say, he was angry because he feared the loss of his job. If he lost his job, then his life would become meaningless, insecure and isolated, with no self-esteem. Yet the anger, the hatred, and the guilt persisted.

In one of the following sessions, Jacob posed the question that surely his anger must have some function if it was so difficult to get rid of it. And, if so, what was it? The anger was so basic that it must have served as some bodily protection, Jacob argued. 'So maybe I cannot get rid of it' he said. I challenged him to scrutinise his present predicament and asks himself where his anger was now? While Jacob acknowledged that his anger had gone, he also knew that it would return at some 'inappropriate' time.

Subsequently, I urged him to examine what harm he had committed to others as a result of his anger. Jacob realised that he managed to stop his anger before he did anything harmful. He knew of a number of irregularities committed by the stranger he hated, but would never have thought of inflicting harm and reporting him. Jacob came to the conclusion that he could not stop the immediate surge of his emotions, but he could become aware of them and stop any consequent action. In his words: 'Anger could otherwise soon get out of hand and one could kill another'.

Meaninglessness

The routine in Jacob's life had changed. Three years previously his mother had died, so his regular weekly visits to her had ceased. It caused Jacob immense distress. Even after three years of grieving it had been difficult for him to overcome his loss.

During a session after a one-week holiday, Jacob recounted the feelings of futility which overwhelmed him during these seven days off work. He spoke of his loneliness and isolation. Even in his flat he found no purpose; he could not indulge in playing or listening to music, nor could he find any purpose in sorting and looking at his erotic catalogues. He could not find any meaning in his current routine. He felt lost and helpless. Therefore, he stayed at home all week. He was also contemplating his advancing age. He felt anxious at the thought of approaching death and dying like his mother. In that session we also considered, as many times before, the possibility of our ending the therapeutic relationship,

Jacob spoke in a tone of equanimity and resignation. He explored this state of futility, which reminded him of the losses in his life, his first love of that fourteen-year-old girl, the loss of his father and mother. He questioned what there was to live for. I was taken aback at Jacob's unusual stance. In my experience, meaninglessness was a sign of depression, which I did not expect of him. Thereafter, I challenged him to investigate how he felt in his present situation in our relationship. I thought he was going to refer again to the ending of the therapy course, but he said he felt contented at that particular moment, because he felt good that he was able to express all his woes and could unburden his mind freely. I urged him to stay with this feeling.

After a while he began reminiscing about various stages of his life that were interwoven with anger, fear, love, joy and other emotions and how all these affected his life. He remembered his childhood love and how it affected his sexual behaviour; the relentless anger toward his two bosses who wanted to belittle him, and then the doctors who wanted to take away his joy. After a considerable silence, I asked him whether he would like to be someone else? In reply, he compared himself to a very close relative of his who was a well-known writer and had a family with children. It was not difficult for Jacob to arrive at a spontaneous, and undisputed conclusion. Despite all his tribulations and anguish, he said he felt content with his present routine and had no other aspirations. What is more, he felt that in his present situation he was happier than the relative who was full of aspirations.

Jacob is still with me in therapy, because we both feel it is important for his life routine that he should able to freely express himself in a trusting environment. Jacob has read this study and is happy for it to be published, although I insisted that events and names would be disguised.

Self Experience

In contrast to Jacob's life, mine has been governed by never-ending aspirations. Yet, there are as many similarities as there is uniqueness in both our lives. For example, during the communist regime in Hungary I was caught in the process of fleeing the country and I was detained for one day for interrogation. They kept me standing against a wall for the whole day. During this seemingly never-ending ordeal, I totally lost my orientation and felt helpless and meaningless. I was convinced that I would be taken to Russia or to Siberia. Yet, I was able somehow to extricate myself from this hopeless mental place. I began to fantasise about entirely inconceivable situations. For instance, I developed a new, alas entirely illusionary, aspiration that I would improve my Russian language in prison. Through this I could become a very useful and a privileged person.

In contrast, Jacob moved out of his meaninglessness by considering his present position without creating new aspirations and found meaning in his routine daily activities. Admittedly, the contexts in which our meaninglessness and our loss of self-esteem manifested themselves were totally different. Yet, exploring these facets of ourselves has revealed the way we existed in a particular situation.

We both protected our self-esteem, although by different means. We both manifested our struggles through our emotions, although the probability is that the manner and intensity of sensing these emotions was unique to each of us.

Just consider how both of us, through our feeling of meaninglessness, disclosed some facets of our world-view. When Jacob felt meaningless, he found some meaning in his present routine. In his work, in his music and in his relationship with me he disclosed his value and behaviour patterns. In the same way, I disclosed my own values and behaviours in that single incident when in my fantasy I created a new aspiration to study Russian and thus become special. I changed my aspirations according to the context of the situation.

Jacob's self-esteem hinged on his positive judgement of music, work, sexuality, and his relationship with me. In my case, self-esteem depended on my positive judgement of knowing a language and creating an ambition. These were my 'meaning' in the context of the situation. Thus, in both of us our aspirations revealed our world-views. In both instances, our behaviour pattern was revealed, which was also part of our world-view. In Jacob's case, his strategy of survival was to preserve the status quo, whereas I created new aspirations.

All other aspects of our world-view, such as sexuality, interpersonal relationships and other emotions are interconnected with each other. Our constraints are not only the existential limits of the world, but also the contextual givens of the situation and they influence our attitude to our value and behaviour patterns. However, each of us employed our individual way of responding in creating our strategies for survival. For both of us, emotions that related to meaninglessness not only manifested our world-views, but also illustrated their connections to our other existential givens. Fear, for example, was connected to other emotions, as well as to our value and behaviour systems and to our self-esteem. All these were in turn further linked to our free will, which because of our circumstances, were limited only to attitudinal choices.

Graph A: Givens of our existence, excluding emotions.

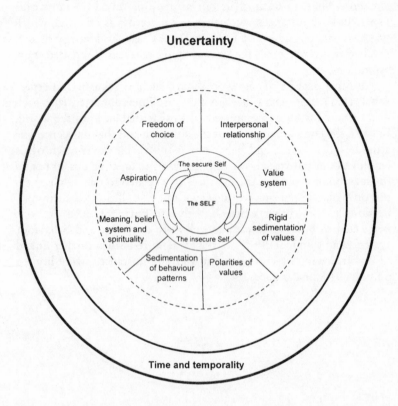

Graph A illustrates the basic givens and the inevitable human reactions which are the universal human characteristics of existing in this world, exemplifying the affinity that links human beings with other human beings – and hence therapists with their clients.

These graphs represent the structure of being in the world between birth and death. The chart is only an approximate illustration and it must not be taken too literally. It was first published in *Existential Time-Limited Therapy: The Wheel of Existence* (1997) and it has been modified since. It may help us realise that, in our work as therapists, a structure of being should be our starting point if we want to understand our clients better. *We are as exposed to the limitations of the world as they are*. Admittedly, this drawing can only convey part of the myriad of human interactions. It may be criticised for not

Graph B: Givens of our existence, including emotions.

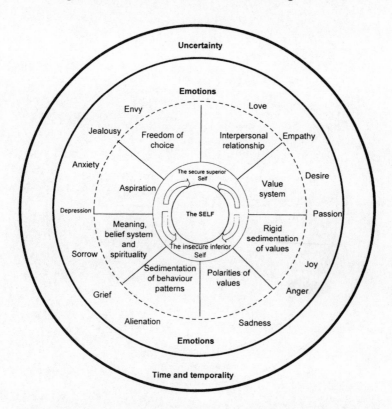

Graph B expands and completes Graph A by demonstrating how emotions may reveal our approaches to our world-view. The emotions in the second wheel are not exhaustive and represent only a small part of the emotional spectrum.

taking into account the infinite differences in the way individuals respond to the uncertainties of life and the endless variety of divergences in experiencing emotions.

I am aware that there are many other ways to represent the structure of our existence. In spite of this, I have experienced that awareness of this graph – which comprises many states of our world-view – has been helpful for me in therapy. It keeps the therapist aware that the relationship with a client is always interwoven with many common denominators.

References

Bandler, R. & Grinder, J. (1979) *Frogs into Princes*. Enfield: Eden Grove Editions

Bentall, R.P. (1992) 'A proposal to classify happiness as a psychiatric disorder' in *Journal of Medical Ethics* 18: 94-98

Boss, M. (1994) *Existential Foundations of Medicine and Psychology*. Northvale, N.J.: Jason Aronson

Buber, M. (1958) *I and Thou*. Edinburgh: T & T Clark

Bugental, J.F.T. (1987) The Art of the New York, London: W.W. Norton Psychotherapist

Cohn, H.W. (1997) *Existential Thought and Therapeutic Practice*: *Introduction to Existential Psychotherapy*. London: Sage

Deurzen-Smith, E. van (1997) *Everyday Mysteries*. London, New York: Routledge

Deurzen-Smith, E. van (1998) *Existential Counselling in Practice*. London, Newbury Park: Sage

Ekman, P. & Davidson, R.J. (1994) *The Nature of Emotion*. New York, Oxford: Oxford University Press

Fell III, J.P. (1965) ?*Emotion in the Thought of Sartre*? New York: Columbia University Press

Frankl, V.E. (1988) *The Will to Meaning* Harmondsworth: Penguin Books

Freud, S. (1984) *The Ego and the Id* Vol.11 Trans. Strachey, J. Harmondsworth: Penguin Books

Freud, S. (1973) *New Introductory Lectures on Psychoanalysis* Vol. 2 Trans. Strachey, J. Harmondsworth: Penguin Books

Friedman, M. (1964) *The Worlds of Chicago Existentialism* London: Chicago University Press

Heidegger, M. (1962) *Being and Time* Oxford: Basil Blackwell

Herink, R. (1986) *The Psychotherapy Handbook* New York, Scarborough: New American Library

Hillman, J. (1961) *Emotion: A Comprehensive Phenomenology of Theories and their Meaning in Therapy* Evanston, Ill.: Northwestern University Press

Husserl, E. (1975) 'Introduction to the Logical Investigation' In (Ed.) Fink, E. A *Draft Of a Preface to the Logical Investigations* (1913) The Hague: Nijhoff

Izard, C.E. (1991) *The Psychology of Emotions* New York, London: Plenum Press

Jasper, K. (1931) *Psychologie der Weltanschauungen* Trans. Frank, M. & Newton, A.Chicago, London: Chicago University Press

Kierkegaard, S. (1944) *The Concept of Dread* Trans. Lowrie, W. Princeton, N.J.: Princeton University Press

Lazarus, R.S. (1991) *Emotion and Adaptation* New York, Oxford: Oxford University Press

Le Doux, J.E. (1993) 'Emotional Networks' in (Ed.) Lewis, M. & Haviland, J.M. *Handbook of Emotions* New York, London: The Guildford Press

Le Doux, J.E. (1994) 'Emotion, Memory and the Brain' in *Scientific American* :June

Lewis, M. (1993) 'Emergence of Human Emotions' in (Ed.) Lewis, M. & Haviland, J.M. *Handbook of Emotions* New York, London: The Guildford Press

Lewis, M. & Haviland, J.M. (1993) *Handbook of Emotions* New York, London: The Guildford Press

May, R. (1977) *The Meaning of Anxiety* New York: Plenum

May, R. (1983) *The Discovery of Being* New York: W.W. Norton

Merleau-Ponty, M. (1962) *Phenomenology of Perception* London: Routledge & Kegan Paul

Nietzsche, F. (1968) *The Will to Power* New York: Vintage Books trans. Kaufmann, W. & Hollingdale, R.J.

Oatley, K. & Jenkins (1996) *Understanding Emotions* Malden, Mass., Oxford: Blackwell Publishers Jenkins, J.M.

Page, S. & Wosket, V. (1994) *Supervising the Counsellor* London, New York: Routledge

Perls, F. (1959) *Gestalt Therapy Verbatim* New York: Bantam Books

Rogers, C. R. (1980) *The Way of Being* Boston: Houghton Mifflin Company

Sartre, J.P. (1958) *Being and Nothingness: An Essay in Phenomenological Ontology* Trans. Hazel Barnes London: Routledge.

Sartre, J.P. (1962) *Sketch for a Theory of Emotions* London: Routledge

Shaw, G.B. (1963) Man and Superman in *Complete Plays with*

Prefaces (Vol. 3:483-686) New York: Dodd, Mead (Original published 1905).

Solomon, R.C. (1993) 'The Philosophy of Emotions' in (Eds) Lewis, M. & Haviland, J.M. *Handbook of Emotions* New York, London: The Guildford Press.

Spinelli, E. (1989) *The Interpreted World* London, Newbury Park: Sage

Spinelli, E. (1994) *Demystifying Therapy* London: Constable

Spinelli, E (1999) 'Réculer pour mieux sauter' in *Journal of the Society for Existential Analysis*

Strasser, F. and Strasser, Y. (1997) *Existential Time-Limited Therapy* Chichester, New York: John Wiley & Sons

Strongman, K.T. (1996) 'Emotion and Memory' in (Eds) Malatesta-Magai, C. & McFaden, S.H. *Handbook of Adult Development and Aging* New York: Academic Press

Strongman, K.T. (1996) The Psychology of Emotion: *Theories of Emotion In Perspective* Chichester, New York: John Wiley & Sons

Yalom, I.D. (1980) *Existential Psychotherapy* New York: Basic Books

Warnock, M. (1962) Preface in Sartre, J.P. *Sketch for a Theory of Emotions* London: Routledge.

Index

SUBJECTS

absolute, 75, 142
accent, 54, 56, 68
achieving, 11, 41
adequate, 7, 23, 143
aggression, 28, 36, 41
Alexander Technique, 113
anger, 23-34, 35-53, 61-3, 123-5,
   128-9, 133-4, 145-8, 160-3
annihilation, 15, 53, 71, 116
appraise, 36, 37, 51
apprehension, 55
approval, 18, 42, 45, 46, 67, 69,
   91, 105, 125, 130, 131, 132,
   153
assumptions, 3, 12, 16, 19, 58,
   120, 143, 159
attitude, 1, 11, 16, 17, 18, 48, 50,
   78, 82, 86, 87, 89, 110, 112,
   114, 120, 143, 159, 165
authority, 42, 43, 92, 119, 123
awareness, 2, 10, 13, 20, 27, 36,
   41, 50, 55, 69, 71, 86, 96, 103,
   105, 137-9, 141, 144, 145, 146,
   149, 151, 153

background, 3, 12, 13, 14, 24, 38,
   41, 54, 55, 56, 64, 67, 68, 71,
   78, 142
belief, 11, 12, 18, 19, 24, 29, 57,
   60, 67, 82, 87, 91, 109, 115,
   117, 122

belittle, 67, 163
bitter, 24
bored, 81, 161
boundaries, 13, 43, 47, 87, 89,
   91, 93, 94, 99, 101, 102, 136
bracket, 152
business, 12, 47, 88, 95, 107, 108,
   141, 142

Cartesian, 7
catharsis, 36, 133
change, 10, 11, 12, 17, 20, 21, 26,
   42, 45, 48, 50, 63, 66, 67, 81,
   82, 87, 93, 98, 100, 102, 103,
   106, 108, 111, 112, 114, 116,
   126
choosing, 17, 87, 126
cluster analysis, 24
cognitive, 19, 23, 26, 64, 122,
   146, 151
commitment, 13, 40, 47, 57, 75,
   83, 93, 109, 136
compassion, 78, 79, 90, 157, 161
compulsion, 42, 113
confidence, 45, 50, 60, 67, 68, 90,
   111, 115
confusion, 24, 128, 129, 134, 136
consciousness, 7, 15, 28, 29, 30,
   32
consistency, 13, 99
consulting room, 13, 32, 38, 43,

56, 88, 93, 103, 161

contempt, 59, 62, 68, 74

control, 17, 23, 25, 27, 28, 29, 36, 45, 51, 66, 97, 113, 123, 140-53, 157, 160

creativity, 55, 81

criticism, 102

death, 7, 53, 54, 55, 72, 85, 87, 138, 163

decision, 57, 71, 103, 127, 129, 150

defences, 153

degree, 13, 17, 20, 46, 55, 76, 95, 103, 156

depression, 12, 16, 45, 86, 91, 94, 99, 102, 122, 163

despair, 40, 53, 58, 62, 87, 101, 122, 123

despise, 56

dialectic, 11

dignity, 147, 150

disgust, 25

disregard, 51

distress, 53, 163

divorce, 33, 142, 148

dread, 53, 56, 89, 91, 106, 130, 131, 160

dream, 61, 62, 63, 73, 81, 106, 150

DSM IV, 122

education, 32, 35, 42, 58, 68, 88, 142

ego, 2, 18, 126

electric, 158

ending, 4, 9, 13, 14, 19, 46, 55, 65, 77, 115, 163, 164

envious, 24, 30, 44, 54, 61

environment, 2, 10, 13, 14, 20,

36, 44, 102, 108, 111, 139, 161, 164

envy, 37, 41

epileptic, 89, 91, 92, 93, 94, 97, 104

equilibrium, 121

existence, 5, 7, 9, 10, 13, 14, 23, 25, 27, 28, 31, 54, 55, 85, 91, 98, 107, 134, 135, 141, 142

existential, 2-4, 7, 8, 9, 12, 16, 19, 24, 30, 34, 38, 54, 55, 71, 73, 75, 79, 86, 123, 124, 128, 129, 134, 137, 138, 146, 147, 150, 165

expectation, 7, 9, 108

extremes, 99, 128, 133, 146

extrovert, 11, 18

facilitate, 15, 19, 27, 36, 61, 129, 140

fail, 143

failure, 37, 42, 49, 63, 80, 94, 102, 143, 150, 153

faint, 25, 101

fear, 3, 18, 25, 28, 41, 43, 53-70, 71, 74, 76, 79, 89, 90, 93, 94, 102, 103, 106, 110, 111, 128, 133, 143-6, 153, 160-3

feedback, 65, 82, 120

food, 15, 107, 108, 113, 153

free will, 21, 51, 165

frustration, 30, 31, 42, 45, 47, 80, 138, 161

Gestalt, 113

givens, 5, 9, 10, 12, 17, 19, 21, 24, 27, 31, 85, 86, 87, 103, 146, 151, 165

guidance, 90, 125, 129

guilt, 3, 42, 71, 73, 74, 75, 76, 77,

78, 79, 80, 82, 89, 91, 105, 144, 146, 147, 148, 162

happiness, 34, 36, 85, 87, 107, 108, 121, 122, 157
happy, 18, 58, 60, 78, 87, 107, 108, 110, 111, 113, 114, 116, 121, 122, 131, 140, 159, 164
harmony, 36, 121, 125, 129, 156
hate, 4, 120, 128, 141, 148, 149, 153
helpless, 30, 77, 79, 109, 110, 116, 157, 163, 164
holiday, 80, 100, 107, 145, 163
hostility, 30
humble, 152
humiliation, 53, 59, 65
humility, 11
hurt, 43, 79, 95, 96, 102

idealism, 7
identification, 5, 15, 67
illness, 93, 157
illusory, 71
imperfection, 135
in the world, 2, 9, 10, 11, 12, 13, 16, 17, 18, 20, 27, 60, 67, 86, 95, 102, 135
inability, 29, 47, 75, 76, 116, 133, 136
inadequacy, 46, 58, 76, 79, 123, 150
inferiority, 35, 40, 41, 74, 151, 161
inhibition, 18
innocence, 15
insecurity, 15, 35, 41, 48, 49, 51, 59, 89, 90, 131, 132, 135, 148, 151
insight, 29, 45, 50, 60, 64, 74, 82,

83, 112, 123, 124, 125, 137
insomnia, 12
intention, 2, 10, 40, 63, 79, 82, 125, 129, 136
intercourse, 89, 98
interpersonal, 9, 10, 11, 13, 14, 16, 19, 50, 89, 91, 94, 165
interpersonal relationship, 9, 13, 19
interpretation, 26, 43, 145
intervention, 14, 15, 45, 47, 59, 60, 61, 63, 67, 79, 81, 88, 114
irritation, 29, 82

jealousy, 37, 103
joke, 72
joy, 3, 4, 17, 25, 26, 30, 36, 42, 53, 72, 75, 86, 87, 108, 111, 112, 113, 120, 121-37, 159, 163
judgement, 38, 151, 152, 164

last session, 43, 46, 65
lazy, 141, 144, 145, 146
libido, 46, 47
limitations, 5, 7, 10, 11, 17, 18, 21, 37, 55, 57, 68, 102, 135
listen, 5, 28, 30, 32, 33, 74, 90, 94, 108, 116, 117, 120
literature, 2, 7, 65
lonely, 35, 86, 87, 117, 160

manifestation, 15, 18, 24, 28, 148
master and slave, 23, 36
masturbation, 89, 91, 100, 102, 111, 158
materialism, 7
mediocrity, 49
metaphor, 23, 44, 91, 106, 134, 157

modular system, 14
motivation, 34, 40, 57, 59, 67, 91

neurotic, 54, 71, 73, 148, 151
nightmare, 85
non-directive counselling, 19

objective, 1, 2, 7, 13, 43, 47, 54,
    62, 111, 126
obliterate, 97, 105
observe, 15, 18, 28, 31, 41, 90
ontological, 9, 12, 13
open-ended, 9, 10, 14, 38, 61, 88,
    156
opportunity, 5, 11, 20, 44, 46, 48,
    50, 74, 79, 82, 108, 120, 122,
    125, 126, 129, 134, 136
outsider, 35, 40, 108

Paradox of Hate, 140
passion, 28, 91, 145
past, 43, 61, 79, 88, 91, 131, 143,
    151
patronise, 67
perfect, 41, 42, 43, 46, 49, 50, 51,
    76, 80, 82, 92, 96, 101, 131
phenomena, 1, 7
phenomenology, 1, 7
philosophy, 5, 7, 9, 23, 155
polarity, 16
posture, 5, 42, 44, 115, 121
potential, 5, 71, 73, 75, 79, 80,
    132, 141, 145, 156
predict, 45
presenting problem, 58, 74, 105,
    160
pressure, 14, 66, 109, 158
pride, 86, 116, 150
pronunciation, 56
psyche, 68, 109

psychoanalytical, 2, 70, 117
psychotherapy, 3, 9, 57, 119, 120

rediscover, 1, 20, 32
reflective, 2, 4, 24, 26, 27, 28, 51,
    142, 143, 146
regret, 71, 95
rejection, 17, 40-1, 43-5, 48, 58-
    60, 63, 74, 91, 94, 97, 100-2,
    116, 131, 146, 152-3, 159
relationship, 1, 7, 9, 11, 13, 15,
    20, 43, 47, 51, 56, 57, 71, 74,
    78-83, 86-91, 94, 102-3, 108-
    13, 119-20, 127, 131, 135-7,
    140-3, 152-3, 157-8, 163-4
resist, 113, 120
retarded, 155, 159
ridicule, 35
rigid, 11-12, 15-16, 20, 30, 42,
    50, 58, 64, 69, 83, 87, 91, 99,
    102, 109-10, 112, 115, 117,
    135-38, 151, 162
risk, 43, 95, 135

sadness, 3, 31, 80, 85-103, 107,
    145, 151, 152, 153, 161
science, 7, 66
sedimentation, 11, 15, 42, 43, 45,
    50, 87, 115, 136, 144, 153
self-construct, 10, 144, 146, 147,
    151
sexuality, 29, 89, 90, 91, 102, 125,
    127, 132, 156, 157, 158, 164,
    165
shame, 3, 14, 29, 58, 59, 63, 64,
    68, 80, 105, 111, 112, 114,
    115, 140
shy, 88
sorrow, 41, 61, 86, 87, 90, 91, 92,
    94, 96, 99, 157

spell, 24, 25, 26
spirituality, 12, 17
spontaneity, 60, 128
strength, 30, 42, 59, 64, 90, 108, 120, 136, 149, 152
structure of being, 10, 11, 13, 18, 20
stuckness, 139
stupid, 141, 144, 145
success, 12, 34, 36, 42, 149, 150, 153
suicide, 99
superior, 30, 37, 44, 46, 49, 50, 51, 53, 58, 146, 160, 161
supervision, 4, 119, 120, 123-4, 128, 133-8, 139, 142-50, 153
support, 20, 36, 38, 61, 83, 99, 119
survival, 11, 12, 16, 17, 41, 59, 112, 113, 150, 165
symbol, 61
system, 11, 12, 15, 17, 45, 50, 68, 74, 87, 91, 101, 112, 115, 121, 123, 131, 135

temper, 33, 34, 44, 123, 142, 145, 149, 161
theory of emotions, 1, 24
therapeutic process, 14, 28, 49, 109, 137
threat, 11, 15, 25, 28, 30, 41, 44, 45, 48, 50, 54, 55, 59, 71, 87, 94, 116, 143, 160

time-limited, 9, 10, 14, 19, 38, 88
tool, 5, 16, 36
transgression, 71
trembling, 25, 54, 72
trepidation, 56, 62, 93, 160
trust, 32, 66, 79, 80, 81, 82, 88, 90, 93, 95, 101, 111, 139, 149, 151
tune, 15, 19, 41, 80, 109

ugly, 40, 42, 45, 46, 110, 128
unaware, 4, 15, 17, 24, 28, 39, 51, 60
uncontaminated, 1, 4, 155
unique, 5, 137, 159, 164
unloved, 62
useless, 92, 96, 100

vacuum bubble, 20
vice, 36, 37, 113
vicious circle, 96
virtue, 37
vulnerability, 54, 62, 63, 66, 68, 116, 123, 140, 161

weakness, 30, 35, 42, 108, 120
weep, 30
woe, 90
working-class, 54, 55, 56, 64, 68
worthlessness, 40, 59

yoga, 19

NAMES

Alexander the Great, 1, 18
Aristotle, 1, 24, 37

Bandler, 1, 4
Bentall, 1, 122
Boss, 1, 10
Buber, 1, 10
Bugental, 1, 10

Cohn, 1, 13

Darwin, 1
Descartes, 1, 24
Deurzen-Smith, 1, 10, 72, 122

Fell, 1, 8, 27
Frankl, 1, 10, 17, 64, 86
Freud, 1, 3, 19, 24, 120

Grinder, 1, 4

Heidegger, 1, 8, 10, 33
Herink, 1, 3
Hillman, 1, 25
Hume, 1, 24
Husserl, 1, 8, 10, 30, 31

Izard, 1, 30, 35

Jasper, 1, 10
Jung, 1, 24

Kierkegaard, 1, 8, 10

Lazarus, 1, 24, 25
Le Doux, 1, 27
Lewis, 1, 27

May, 1, 8, 10, 35, 55, 72
Merleau-Ponty, 1, 8, 10

Napoleon, 1, 18
Nietzsche, 1, 8, 10

Oatley, 1, 27

Page, 1, 120
Perls, 1, 3, 19, 37

Rogers, 1, 8, 20, 122

Sartre, 1, 3, 10, 18, 25, 27, 28, 30, 31, 33
Shaw, 1, 122
Solomon, 1, 24
Spinelli, 1, 4, 8, 10, 15, 16, 32, 72
Strasser, A., 4, 140-1
Strasser, F., 1, 18, 56, 125, 129

Warnock, 1, 30, 33
Watson, 1, 24
Wosket, 1, 120

Yalom, 1, 10, 55, 72